AF540825

Correlates of Socialization

Dr. KANDI JAYASREE
M.Sc., M.Ed., M.Phil., Ph.D
Lecturer in Physical Science Education
St. Joseph's College of Education for Women
5th Line, Shyamala Nagar, Guntur - 522 006

Editor

Dr. DIGUMARTI BHASKARA RAO
R.V.R. College of Education
D-43, Srinivas Nagar
Guntur - 522 006, Andhra Pradesh

1999
DISCOVERY PUBLISHING HOUSE
NEW DELHI

First Published 1999

ISBN 81-7141-517-2

Published by
DISCOVERY PUBLISHING HOUSE
4831/24, Ansari Road, Prahlad Street
Darya Ganj, New Delhi - 110 002 (*INDIA*)
Phone: 327 92 45
Fax: 91-11-325 34 75

Printed at:
Arora Offset Press
Laxmi Nagar, Delhi 110 092.

Preface

Socialization is a continuous learning process associated with inter-action between individuals. It is a process of value both to the individual who gets socialized and the group which socializes him. It makes an individual aware of the roles to be played by him in the society, teaches the basic skills of social life, develops a sense of belongingness to a group, disciplines the expulsive behaviour through approvals and disapprovals, instils aspirations, creates self-image, gives poise and self-confidence, develops proper adjustment strategies, and refines the personality. In the present scientific and technological world, the attitude towards science and scientific attitude contribute much to the socialization phenomenon of life along with other factors of socialization.

Identifying the importance of socialization in the life of an individual and the role of attitude towards science and scientific attitude in the process of socialization, a study has been conducted. In the study, a significant percentage of sample—adolescent students studying in junior colleges—were showing high socialization ability. The traits, viz., socialization ability, attitude towards science and scientific attitude, were directly associated with each other. As the improvement in socialization ability helps a student to successfully participate in the educational process for better prospects, it becomes a dire duty of all agencies of socialization to adequately socialize him. Also, the individuals and institutions must interact with each other in perfect blend to fabricate a meaningful social harmony.

We express our thanks to Prof. T.J. Rajendra Prasad, Mr. G. Sundara Rao, Mr. K. Jagannadha Rao, Dr. M. Shyama Sundara Rao, Dr. J. Prasanth Kumar, Mr. Mastan Reddy and Dr. M. Vanaja for their valuable support at every stage of this product.

Dr. D. Bhaskara Rao
Dr. K. Jayasree

Contents

1

Introduction

Education is a process through which the inborn qualities or latent powers of the child are improved and unfurled, so that his personality is developed.

SOCIAL AIM OF EDUCATION

Dewey (1963) highlighting the sociological importance of the educational process holds that

> All education proceeds by the participation of the individual in this social consciousness of the race.

The preamble of National Education Policy (1986) states that

> An ideal system of education should enable individuals to know and develop to the fullest, their physical and intellectual potentialities, and promote their awareness of social and human values, so that they can develop a strong character and live better lives and function as responsible members of the society. It is by transforming human being that social transformation can be brought about.

It is important that education has to take into account the social aim also as the social values, mores and milieus make the individual socialised.

Rose (1962) has aptly concluded as

> ...individuality is of no value and personality is a meaningless term apart from the social environment in which they are developed and made manifest.

The very nature of the Indian culture based on peace, fraternity, toleration and fellow-feeling is conducive to a congenial synthesis of the social and individual aims of education.

The basic unit of any society is the individual. Society is a structured organisation and it constitutes several institutions and organisations. Man is a part and parcel of the society. Individuals and institutions interact with one another resulting in social harmony and peace.

The society is interested in making each individual a valuable asset. Education is an instrument which brings about socially desirable changes in the individual and enables him to live happily in the society.

It is necessary that the child has to be trained to become an efficient adult. The characterisation of a child takes place mostly in the school. School, being a miniature society, tries to give proper education so as to develop an integrated personality of the individual. The school is said to be an embryonic community which reflects all features of the society. It is the formal agency of education, that systematically transmits not only beliefs, traditions, customs, attitudes, and values but also ways of living.

SOCIALIZATION PROCESS

Socialization can be defined in terms of the learning process associated with interaction between and among persons. It is also defined as an interacting process between the individual and his environment, through which, the individual becomes a person.

Dewey (1963) says that

> Any education given by a group tends to socialise its members. But the quality and values of the socialisation

depends upon the habits and aims of the groups.

As such, socialization is a process which is of value both to the individual who gets socialized, and the group which socializes him. Further, socialization is a continuous process. It begins from the moment the child becomes responsive to his environment and goes on till the end of his life. It is pronounced in completely new social situations and groups.

The process of socialization takes place in two ways (a) deliberate and (b) unconscious.

In deliberate socialization, techniques of praise and reproof, reward and condemnation, etc., are used. Emphasis on cleanliness, promptness, obedience, learning the skill of language, religious observations, etc., are illustrations of deliberate socialization.

Identification with great people, film actors, school teachers, political leaders, influential relations, imitation of mannerisms, speech habits, etc., are illustrations of unconscious socialization.

Musgrave (1979) opines that

> Prior preparation for socialization is called anticipatory socialisation.

The range of behaviour tolerated in any role is usually quite wide. At this stage the mother in the main has the task of providing rules and targets for her child. This initial stage is called as 'psychological symbiosis'.

Often the main method of socializing the child would seem to be the regular presence of a role model, to be initiated, who has power or is highly valued and who persistently behaves in a consistent manner. This is necessary for a child to be properly socialized.

FACTORS CONTRIBUTING TO SOCIALIZATION

Development of social conformity, social adjustment, social intelligence, and positive moral character are the important factors involved in socialization.

Social Conformity

Social conformity takes two forms—acquiescence and conventionality. Conformity does not begin in adolescence. Children are highly sensitive to group opinions and try to conform to the beliefs and behaviour of the peer group. But, conformity becomes stronger in adolescence. At that time, the opinions of others especially of one's own age group, are of immense importance. Conformity to the group is more often expressed in behavioural changes than in opinion changes.

So every child has a conformity to his group in order to be accepted by the group. The process here is identification.

School should become 'a secondary model' for the child to follow and should teach the principles of democratic living. If the teacher makes the child question himself, the causes of prejudices, he may correct himself and try to come out of his various types of prejudices because of which proper socialization may take place.

Social Adjustment

Social adjustment among adolescents and youths is measured by the degree of popularity in the peer group. It means achieving satisfactory status with his peers. The school as a socializing agency, helps the children in achieving the social adjustment.

Elizabeth B. Hurlock (1955) is of the opinion that

> There are some important sub factors which determine the social acceptability and in turn the social adjustment. They are first impressions, personal appearance, health, social, economic status, degree of activity, possession of skills, family relationships, size of family, proximity, length of acquaintance, acceptance of group values and social insight.

Social Intelligence

George, H. Mead (1934) observes that

> Taking the role of another person or putting one self into the other, is sometimes referred to as 'social intelligence'.

This role taking involves anticipation. The anticipatory response is facilitated by the development of language, child enacts the role of another anticipating the standard role of other people. This helps in his ordinary interaction with the other people. This is why in which he internalises the norms in the behaviour of other people. This helps him to guide his own behaviour in terms of other people. By this process the behaviour of other people becomes predictable.

Elizabeth B Hurlock (1986) said that

> People also learn some social skills. One of the most important social skills a person has, is an opportunity to learn 'social insight' or the ability to put oneself in the 'psychological shoes' of another and perceive things from his frame of reference, which leads to better social participation because of which proper socialisation takes place in the individual.

Elizabeth B Hurlock (1955) is of the opinion that

> Social competency or social intelligence plays an important role in the kind of an social adjustment the adolescent makes. It gives the adolescent poise and self confidence traits that are of great value in any social situation.

Positive Moral Character

Ultimately much of child's social behaviour (and an adult's too) is determined by ethical ideas about what is right and what is wrong. Although social rules and moral ideas can be inculcated through learning, children seem to go through stages of moral development that are relatively independent of specific training and specific roles.

The child should be given proper training for the development of positive moral character. The person who learns a socially acceptable code of moral values and accepts this code as a guide to his behaviour is more secure, more confident of his ability to live up to the code, and more likely to be a comfortable and well adjusted person. A person of positive moral character knows how to behave properly in the society, how to make proper social interactions, the do's and don'ts of social living, and also knows how to work for the welfare of the society.

AGENCIES OF SOCIALIZATION

Every society has needs, aspirations and goals of life based on the life style of its people. These needs, aspirations and goals of life of a society are realized through a number of organisations like the home, the religious institution, the school, the youth clubs, the mass media, etc., called as agencies of education. These are organisations of society, which preserve and perpetuate social customs, traditions, beliefs, values, etc., while satisfying the primary needs of an individual. The social agencies are instruments of social stability and social change.

There are two types of agencies, namely, formal and informal. Among the formal agencies of education family is the first social institution in the history of human society. It is the fundamental unit of society, and is the centre of emotional life for a person.

By the time the child starts to school he has already acquired many of his social behavioural patterns, has developed a personality, has a body of habits, knowledge, and attitudes that are useful for his future adjustment.

A family has seven important functions: affectional economic, educational, protectional, recreational, family, and religious functions. In this modern age the functions of the family have undergone changes, for example: economic, educational and recreational functions are shared by other agencies.

Throughout the history of human civilisation religious organisations have played a significant role as agencies of socialization. They rendered unique, distinguished, and specialised services to the society in the socialization of its members.

There are innumerable agencies of socialization either spontaneously formed or set up deliberately in the society. They range from temporary play groups of small children in remote corners of the world, to world bodies such as United Nations Organisations. These agencies serve to fulfil many individual and societal needs, through their activities and programmes. They also incidentally and in certain respects deliberately, serve to transmit the social heritage of the group. The influence of many of these agencies on the personality development of individuals is profound and lasting.

The State itself through its widespread machinery, may act as an agency of socialization. Television also acts as an agency of socialization, as it is being very much in use. Press also acts as an agency of socialization.

As said before, school is an important socialization to serve certain individual and societal needs which are originally designed and established by the society. The school became the integral and central organ of a community for socialization of younger generation.

The community at large is usually a complex one in terms of members, structure, status, roles and relationships. The school is a simple society in all these aspects.

In the interest of a smooth transition from childhood to adulthood, it is necessary to familiarise children with the existing norms of the adult world. Secondary, the norms of behaviour prevailing in the present system may undergo change in the course of time. The school has to take into consideration the changes in the society, and behaviour patterns should be introduced in the schools so that the young children may get familiar with the emerging values and become fit to adjust to the future society. This type of socialization is very relevant to the school as social agency.

Of the various agencies of socialization, school is a highly dependable systematised and specialised agency. It is a platform wherein many conflicts arising out of generation gaps, culture-lags, changing norms, etc., are peacefully resolved. The process of socialization involves the various social roles which the individual has to take in order to fulfil the expectations of the society consequently it would be an exaggeration to think that any particular influence at home, in the neighbourhood, or in the school will influence the individuals exclusively.

DEVELOPMENT STAGES IN SOCIALIZATION

The transformation of a non-social neonate into a social adult is the fundamental fact in the process of socialisation.

Kuppuswamy (1971) opines that

> The infant is born as an non-social biological being. He grows up to be a socialised adult. It is due to social experience that a biological being becomes a human being.

From birth to two weeks, the stage is called Neonate or New born.

Crow and Crow (1964) say that

> The neonate is helpless as a self-maintaining and self protecting organism. All of his physical needs are being met. Gradually, he learns to participate, voluntarily and with increasing skill, in such activities as eating, eliminating, sleeping, crawling, walking and running.

A baby in the age range of 'two weeks to two years' is said to be Infancy.

Crow and Crow (1964) also opine that

> Most infants have achieved some simple awareness of others by the time they reach their third month. An infant seems to be able to distinguish between his mother and his father, giving special attention to his mother smiling at her as he focusses his eyes upon her. The very young child appears to gain some awareness of others before he achieves awareness of himself as an entity in his total small environment.

We find a gradual increase in the infant's social awareness. Kuppuswami (1984) opines that

> The earliest pressures of socialisation are applied to the infant in the area of feeding. Regularity in satisfying the hunger drive is looked upon as very important step in socializing the infant.

Kuppuswami (1971) also feels that

> His interest in other children increases as he grows older. There are manifestations of aggressive behaviour when he sees another person possessing the object he desires.

According to Buhler even by 8 months the child expresses satisfaction and pleasure in triumphing over a rival.

Kuppuswamy (1984) opines that

> As the child grows older overt aggression decreases, inner

> controls are learned, more socially acceptable ways of solving conflicts and frustrations are learnt and rules governing 'civilized' behaviour are incorporated and internalized.

In this infancy stage, parents have a great role to play in the socialization of a child.

A child in the age range of two to six years is said to be in early childhood.

From the second to fourth year the child shows extreme dependence on specific individuals like the mother, father and others in the household. As the child grows older there is an increase in independent behaviour and the child will be sent to the nursery school.

Independence promotes good peer relationship. It appears that independence is a sign of security, and it enables the child to function autonomously and promotes effort towards personal accomplishment and attainment of goals

Children in the age group of six to twelve years are said to be in the late Childhood.

Crow and Crow (1964) opine that

> The child's various attitudes and activities that have social impact upon the progress of developing personality gradually serve to motivate his maturing behaviour. Among these social impact activities and attitudes are: laughter, play, friendship, and group contacts.

Children's play activity gives evidence of their increasing social consciousness.

Crow and Crow (1964) also feel that

> The friendships of elementary school age children are formed on very much the same basis as adult friendship, although age (or) growth status is much more important with children than it is with adults.

Similarity in age, grade, social class, and proximity are some of the factors based on which friendships are made.

Crow and Crow (1964) further emphasize that

> Among the members of both sexes, friendships that begin during childhood continue for many years. In some cases they last the life time. As children grow older, group formation for play or forms of activity becomes relatively more fixed. Towards the end of the elementary school years, school and neighbourhood groups become increasingly more stable. The groups that form during late childhood are usually organised on a one-sex basis and often include elaborate organizational and admission rituals. Childhood interests gradually take on a more social character. Group formation activity may constitute an excellent means of promoting the socializing process.

A child in the age range of twelve to fourteen years is said to be in early adolescence.

Crow and Crow (1964) say that

> Like their younger brothers and sisters, adolescents need status, security, affection and independence. The adolescent seeks an appropriate social role for himself and strives to experience satisfying relationships with peer and adult associates.

Herbert Sorenson is of the opinion that

> Adolescents, especially boys band themselves together into clubs and groups and hence this age is called gang age, whereas childhood is called as pre-gang age. The clubs and gangs of adolescents are on more permanent footing because, their interest do not change so frequently as those of children and the object of these clubs is mostly social.

Kuppuswami (1984) says that

> The most important developmental task of adolescence according to Erikson, is the search for and the achievement of sense of identity. Becoming independent of parents and gaining acceptance of peers are important steps in achieving a sense of personal identity.

The choice of and preparation for a career is another crucial step in the process.

Late adolescence occurs between fifteen to eighteen years. In this stage increased hetero-sexual interest is developed. There comes a lively interest in members of the other sex which is the most marked change in the social behaviour of adolescence. The peer group also has greater influence now than the home.

B. Kuppuswamy (1984) feels that

> An adolescent tries to extend his knowledge by more extensive reading and is capable of hypothetic—deductive and inductive reasoning. This is the age at which he chooses an occupation or a course of studies which lead to an occupation. He seeks meaning in life and builds up a sense of values. There is greater desire for freedom and self-direction.

A major problem of the school is to control circumstances so that, the individual student will learn how to get along with people; as friends in school and neighbourhood play a role of great importance in the formation of his pattern of social behaviour and attitudes.

Elizabeth B. Hurlock (1955) opines that

> This young adolescent has three 'social worlds' which are of equal importance to him. The first consists of his family. Many of the social contacts for work and play are with his parents, brothers, and sisters and other relatives. The school provides the second social world for the young adolescent, while the third consists of a small closed world of intimate friendship with one or two individuals of his sex, whom he regards as his 'best friends' and with whom he associates in many of his activities and with whom he shares his thoughts, hopes and worries.

Adolescents usually believe that their peers understand them better than their parents do. Added to this, adolescents being sensitive to the behaviour of their parents express their opinions concerning them to others. So one should not judge the adolescent behaviour from adult standards.

Moreover, in this period, individual's interests widen to

include not only his own welfare and that of his family but also the welfare and activities of other persons and group. If these interests are properly catered for, he will become a good citizen. Schools and parents have greater responsibility in understanding the adolescent properly. They can make him choose his peer group properly because peers have an immense effect on the socialization of the child.

An individual in the age range of eighteen and above is an adult.

Herbert Sorenson says that

> Organisation into groups is not limited to youth. In adulthood both men and women band themselves together in many ways for economic and social purposes. People were described by the older psychologists as having a gregarious instinct because of their tendency to be together. Certain springs of action such as the desire to obtain security and a feeling of personal work also cause adults to organise. These organisations of adults have much in common with those of their youth.

Elizabeth Hurlook (1958) further says that

> In contrast to the late adolescent, adult has four 'social words'. They consists of the home, the school or college, his friends and his job. His relationships with his family are of less importance to him socially than they were when he was young, while his social contacts with members of the social group are stronger. Here he selects a circle of friends that serve as the basis for the major part of his social life. His third social world consists of a group of intimate friends of both sexes, from which he eventually selects one member of the opposite sex with whom he goes steady. The people he associates with, in his job are less important to him socially than the three other social worlds.

OUTCOMES AND VALUES OF SOCIALIZATION

Socialization inculcates basic disciplines ranging from toilet habits to the method of science. Socialization disciplines impulsive behaviour through social approvals and disapprovals. The dos and don'ts of life are learnt through socialization.

Socialization instils aspirations, especially on the part of the younger generation by providing illustrations of great lives, great behaviour forms, great thought and ideas.

It is through socialization that the individual becomes aware of and learns the roles he has to play in the society. How to be a leader, a follower, a pupil, a teacher, etc., are illustrations of such role-playing; such socialization also specifies the virtues, feelings, attitudes, and personality traits proper to the role. Students should be alert, eager, industrious, etc., teachers should be patient, sympathetic, humble, sacrificing, etc., enlisted men shall be obedient, army officer should be aloof, doctors should be kind, etc., are only are only illustrations of such specification of roles.

Socialization teaches the basic skills of social life how to write letters, use of telephone, order of dinner, stand at a prayer, work in a library, etc., are illustrations of such social skills.

Socialization creates a 'self-image'. The concept of 'I' is developed through socialization. The child comes to learn his unique qualities, potentialities, and individualities in comparison with those of others. It is also drilled into the thinking process of the child.

Socialization develops a 'we-feeling', a sense of belongingness to a group. It is through socialization that an individual identifies himself with the achievements of a group.

Cultural values and norms govern individual behaviour through the process of socialization. Both the family and the school transmit some of the culture's dominant values and practices. Without the process of socialization, societies would not endure in any consistent form.

Clifford T. Morgan (1978) states that

> Socialization involves a combination of instruction and imitation. The learning which accompanies socialization is so pervasive that we are not always aware of it.

Tables 1.1 and 1.2 explains the influencing agencies of socialization and the outcomes of socialization ability of an individual.

Table 1.1: ***Agencies of Socialization***

Agencies of Socialization	*Development Stages*	*Outcomes*
Home Especially Mother	Infant	Basic Disciplinee (for anticipatory Socialization)
Home School	Child	Social impact attitudes and activities, Basic learning skills, Basic personality patterns.
Home School or College Peer Group Mass Media	Adolescent	Attitudes values, Personality pattern and self concept Physical Characteristics, Knowledge skills, Achievement, and Vocational interests.
Home Peer Group Mass Media Religious Agencies	Adult	Selection of mate Selection of proper vocation, Characterization, High knowledge skills Integrated personality development, verbal expression.

Outcomes of Social Adult

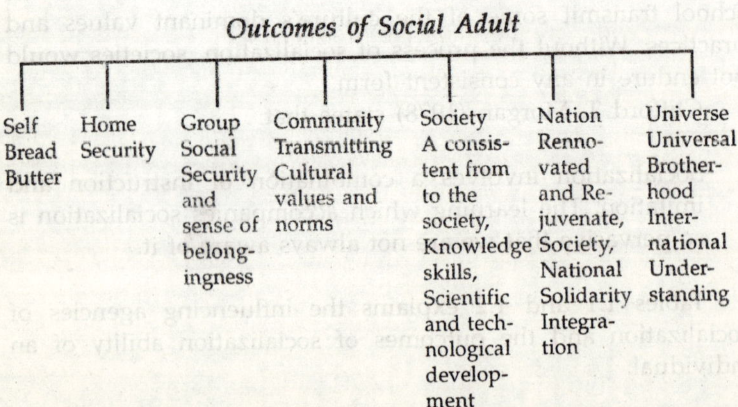

Table 1.1 depicts the influencing agencies if socialization and outcomes during developmental stages.

Socialization ability facilitates two important benefits, namely, Individual and Contributory.

Table 1.2

Outcome of Socializing Ability of an Individual

Individual benefits (Personal Possessions)	Contributory benefits (Theoretical constructs)
1. Bread and Butter	1. Renovated, and Reconstructed Society
2. Security	2. Scientific and Technological Development
3. Social Security and sense of belongingness	3. National Solidarity and Integration
4. Transmitting Cultural Values and Norms	4. Universal Brotherhood
5. Knowledge Skills	5. International Understanding

Table 1.2 shows the outcomes of socialization ability of an individual.

IMPORTANCE OF SOCIALIZATION IN ADOLESCENCE

Socialization is one of the important functions at all levels. In the fast expanding world, the child interacts with people in the environment and society. In the interests of smooth transition from child-world to adult-world it is necessary to familiarise children with the existing norms of adult-world.

Education has to be the chief instrument of society in cleaning the social life of undesirable norms. One of the primary purposes of education is to aid individuals to adjust to personal, school and economic problems. The combined influences of school-cultural demands, the home situation, the social class status and other forces in the adolescent environment operate to produce a well adjusted or poorly adjusted personality.

At the centre of socialization process he is faced with the problem of developing a satisfactory identity or self concept out of interaction with others. Boys and girls gradually develop social feeling while working or playing. By studying friendships in adolescence we can better understand the various aspects that contribute to their complex social maturation.

The adolescent period is very critical in terms of social adjustments and maturation. In making the transition to adult hood many developmental tasks are to be learned by the adolescent. Of these, desiring and achieving socially responsible behaviour is one, through which, he learns how to behave in a socially approved manner according to the taboos and customs and value systems of the society. The socialization process facilitates this type of learning which influences the degree of success the person achieves in life.

The adolescent's physical and psychological development, attitudinal developments, his ambitions, development of value system may in turn be affected by the socialization process he has undergone. The interaction between these can lead to the complete development of the individual.

The adolescent has three different worlds, of which the peer group and school may have greater influence on him than home. Adolescents usually take peers into their confidence more than the parents and feel secure. It is here he learns the social skills that are necessary. School also has a great role to play in acquiring the social skills.

Goodwin Watson (1966) says that

> It is impossible for a child, even if he could survive physically in isolation to develop moral human attributes except through social interaction.

Better socialization ability makes a person popular, energies boosted, and ego-satisfied, sacrifice their needs at the cost of social needs and work for the welfare of the society. It also leads to better achievement and better self concept, which in turn leads to proper marital health and other psychological adjustments which are very important for an adolescent world who is on his way to adult hood. An adolescent world is different from others and he is full of energies and ambitions for future life and develops positive value system.

Through this socialization process he should be able to cope with adolescent problems. Selecting or choosing good friends and proper social interaction with them develops socialization ability in adolescent, which can show an automatic solution for all the adolescent problems.

The adolescent has a problem in getting his role clearly defined. This creates problems with respect to his identity, what Erikson calls the "identity crises" in adolescence. The persons who have proper social intelligence develop social skills necessary to overcome this identity crisis. Satisfactory adult life depends upon the socialization of sex so that the biological and affectional aspects are combined in an optional manner. This will promote an ideal interaction between the pair in married life. A socialized child develops a sense of personal identity, sexual identity, occupational identity and do not have any role confusion.

Lack of socialization leads to socially undesirable behaviour, unnecessary fear, excessive inhibition, excessive aggressiveness and violence, inability to learn, failing in the essential tasks of 7Rs (Reading, Writing, Arithmetic, Social relations, Recreation, Responsibilities and Rights) which in turn prevent the development of an adequate and healthy personality.

Failure in socialization can lead to different forms of delinquency and also lead to failure in the development of conscience. The sense of "alienation" has been increasing in the recent decades because of the lack of social skills. Though alienation may not lead to delinquency, it appears to be at the basis of the "breathnik" movement and the "hippie" movement with its drug addiction, etc.

Because of lack of socialization a person develops hatred towards society, revengeful, cruel and in order to boost his ego tries to do anti-social activities or show bossism or become gang leader.

Attitudinal Development during Adolescence

An attitude denotes an adjustment of the individual towards some selected person, group or institution. An attitude results in a state of preparation or a state of readiness to respond in a particular manner under particular circumstances.

Attitudes may be formed towards persons or group of persons; towards the products of human interaction. These products of human interaction may be the technological devices or they may be the values or norms of a group.

The person's attitude towards the role he is expected to play affects how he plays the role, he feels about being expected to play it.

Since the attitude of members of the social group toward a person moulds his self-attitudes, the person who experiences favourable social attitudes, can be expected to be self-acceptant.

As attitudes define what is to be preferred, expected and desired and, what is desirable and what should be avoided in terms of its consequence, we can say an attitude is goal directed. Attitudes may be referred to as sociogenic motives. Attitudes arise out of the socialization of an individual in a group.

Clifford T. Morgan (1978) opines that

> From birth to puberty children's attitudes are shaped primarily by their parents.
>
> During the period from 12 to 30, most of the person's attitudes take final form and there after change little. This has been called the critical period (Sears 1969)—the period during which attitudes crystallize. During this period three main factors are at work: peer influences information from news media and other sources, and education.

An adolescent's attitudes vary quite a bit, and they are not yet strongly held. The most important change is in the area of social attitudes and behaviour which determines the stage of sexual maturation.

It is at this stage proper education is necessary to develop proper attitudes which in turn help to have a proper outlook towards life.

Education should promote in the raising generation those knowledges, skills and attitudes, which help the process of modernisation.

The school helps to bring to bear on the individual those influences that stimulate and assist him, primarily by his own efforts, to develop to the maximum degree consistent with his capacities. In other words, school offers activities and employs procedures through which the individual is encouraged to make the most of himself.

Of all the adolescent's attitude developments, attitude towards science and scientific attitude are important and useful.

SCIENTIFIC ATTITUDE

The qualities imbibed by the learner through learning science are of great value.

One of the chief aims of science teaching is to develop certain scientific discipline or attitude. The formation of attitudes is a process that starts right from the very beginning in the immediate environment provided by the parents, peer group, neighbourhood, school and society at large.

Collin Gauld (1980) opines that

> The scientific attitude represents the motivation which converts the knowledge of facts and skills in the use of scientific method into action and refers to a 'willingness' to use scientific procedures and methods. It may best be described as "an attitude to ideas and information to particular ways of evaluating them" a formulation which distinguishes it from an attitude to science or scientists on the one hand and from an ability to carry out scientific procedures on the other.

The scientific attitude is applicable to nearly every situation an individual may encounter in the process of acquiring knowledge in life situations. It is closely allied to critical thinking, and it is developed through the study of science as well as other subject matter areas.

National Society of the Study of Education says scientific attitude is "open minded, a desire of accurate knowledge, confidence in procedure for seeking knowledge, and the expectation that the solution of the problem will come through the use of verified knowledge". Scientific attitudes are simply elements in the philosophy of science. They are assumptions and rules of practice which have been formulated consciously and deliberately, or at least have been subjected to searching criticism since their formulation, they are neither sacrosanct nor necessary. They are convenient and fruitful only. The scientific attitude is unified state of mind.

Collin Gauld (1980) also states that

> The scientific attitude as it appears in science education embodies the adoption of a particular approach for solving problems, for assessing ideas and information or for making decisions. Using this approach evidence is collected and evaluated objectively, so that the idiosyncratic prejudices of the one making the judgement do not intrude. All available evidence is carefully weighed before the decision is made. If the evidence is considered to be insufficient, then judgement is suspended. Unless there is enough information to enable a decision to be made. A person to follow this procedure is said to be motivated by the science educator as some one who makes decisions solely on the basis of the weight of empirical evidence.

An individual who has learned the scientific attitude and makes use of it does not jump to conclusions. He is patient and reserved in his judgement. In considering a situation or a problem, he studies all aspects of it, looking at every side of it, before approaching the study with a minimum of prejudice or bias. Although he may have previous knowledge, he will not have preconceived notions, unless they have basis in his objective understanding of the problem.

The persons who possesses the scientific attitude has no time for old wive's tales, rumours or superstitions. He is a person of caution who observes carefully before coming to a conclusion. He is ready and willing to change his ideas when he observes new evidence that he can accept as valid.

The scientific attitude is reflected in the individual who: 1. Bases his actions, thoughts and conducts on the best knowledge that is available to him. 2. Suspends reaching conclusions and forming judgements when reliable and objective information is lacking or until such time as he has the opportunity to study such information.

Carefully planning is one of the most helpful ways of guiding students in the development of such an attitude. The proper development of scientific attitude is possible mainly through conscious attempts during science teaching. By adopting scientific attitudes and transferring these to situation in every day life, students can be expected to be more tolerant of other's point of view and to be more successful in living and working along side with other people.

ATTITUDE TOWARDS SCIENCE

The study of modern science mobilise man's consciousness, his potentialities, love and understanding, which help to have proper human relations.

The study of science also gives opportunity for the development of favourable traits of human character.

In a modernized or modernising society the attributes of modernity are manifested at two levels—at the level of the individual and at the level of society. Inherently the individuals of such society have objective and scientific mind, and a mobile personality. Their mind is operational and critical. It is free from scepticism, inhibitions, and complexes and callous elements of tradition. It has empathy, that is the capacity to see self in other's situational and structural choices.

According to Karl Pearson (1900)

> The classification of facts, the recognition of their sequence and relative significance is the function of science and the habit of forming a judgement upon these facts unbiased by personal feeling is characteristic of what may be termed the scientific frame of mind.

The architect of the modern world is science. The aim of science is to find out the laws of nature. It is more exact to say that the aim of workers in science is to find out the laws of nature. Science is a group of laws, based on observation, and proved correct by experiment.

The important reasons for teaching science are its usefulness to the country and usefulness to the individual.

Owen (1964) is of the opinion that

> A modern state requires men with scientific training, such as doctors, chemists and engineers. These men must start their science sooner or later, and the sooner the better. If the schools do not provide science, then many boys may never have a chance of finding out if they like the subject.

The government of modern states make use of science. In nearly every country the department of agriculture, education, health, police, posts and telegraphs, roadways and surveys, employ scientists. These departments send out orders, many of which will be the result of scientific work, and these orders have to be carried out by officials, merchants and farmers. If they do not understood, the orders will be carried out badly, or not at all, so some knowledge of science is important, to everybody.

A few people use science to earn their living. But they live in a world where science is important. Almost everybody enjoys learning science, because it deals with things they wonder about. An individual man who knows nothing about the discoveries of biology, chemistry and physics in the last three hundred years cannot be called properly educated. Besides, the most important of all the reasons for learning science is that it has a value in character training.

Because of the above reasons every literate person needs to develop and possess a positive Attitude to science.

The history of science in recent centuries the history of the triumph of the spirit of free inquiry over mere opinion, untested belief, prejudice and dogma.

NEED FOR THE STUDY

Once the child is being socialized in a proper manner, he knows how to live in this world. In addition to socialization, advancement of knowledge is another important aim of education. Only when the person is having a proper attitude towards science, he can aspire to be a knowledgeable person. He also realises and appreciates the fundamental principles of science which are essential to effective living in today's world. Hence, to have a proper attitude towards science is very important and this may also be required for socializing the individual.

As already discussed, every individual needs socialization ability, positive attitude towards science, and a better level of scientific attitude. They are useful for effective functioning in the society. Scientific attitude is an outcome of science education. Science, when it is taught in a democratic and social atmosphere is known to help in the development of Scientific attitude. Positive attitude to science is developed through education, media, and technological social environment.

The importance of the three traits, common social components, common origins necessitates a combined study of these three traits in post adolescent students. With the assumption of association of these three traits, studies on student population are necessary.

A two way relationship between the traits is assumed. A individual with high scientific attitude is likely to possess positive Attitude towards science and vice versa.

An individual with high scientific attitude is likely to possess high Socialization ability and vice versa.

An individual with high socialization ability is likely to possess positive attitude towards science and vice versa.

Human behaviour is varied and complex and perhaps it is unrealistic to expect a dozen or so factors to provide an adequate description of it. Moreover an adolescent's attitude vary quite a bit and they are not yet strongly held.

The child's framework of attitudes does not consists of a single functioning entity but is composed of a complex of many traits or characteristics, that are more or less integrated.

These traits are always being affected by many factors in different stages. For example, personality trait, Attitude towards science, scientific attitude, socialization, holding on to value system are some of the traits which influence the growth and development of adolescent.

In spite of the known natural fact that most of the traits tend to develop normally, it is also seen that when a traits is influenced by certain factors, or a trait is being consciously developed through the process of education in an individual then there is every probability that trait distribution, will not be normal in that population. If the traits have grown in the same areas or of same origin than they may be developed in a planned manner.

Some of the traits like socialization ability, Scientific attitude, influence of science on individual may be developed like this.

The socialization ability is very important for a person, to enable to make one self adjusted to the society properly, to learn adequate skills and techniques necessary for the individuals, and also to learn proper attitudes, values, norms that give them proper place in the society and also personal identity or security in the group.

A knowledge of relationship between the traits will be educationally useful because it may result in developing classroom strategies, help in planning proper co-curricular activities. It can also help in developing guidance principles for adolescents.

As attitudes are always functional and also emotionally satisfying, similarity of attitudes may be one of the important determinant of socialization. It will be very useful to know whether there is any relationship between socialization ability and attitude.

Moreover child has to be socialized into the direction of prevailing attitudes. In the modernized society, where tremendous scientific technological development is taking place, it is of importance to find out if there is any relationship between socialization ability and attitudes, especially attitude towards science and scientific attitude, which are very essential for the present day Indian society. If one could find the relationship between these two areas, it is easy to plan to bring about a change in one area which leads to a change in another area also. For example, if socialization ability has a direct relationship to scientific attitude, then there is every possibility to improve the socialization ability of the child through scientific attitude. One can find out the common measures to be followed to improve both. Hence there is a need for the study of this area.

With the knowledge of social structure of the class and group, it will be possible for a teacher to plan to change the students' attitudes. It is a known fact that due to socialization, the child develops not only the desirable in group attitudes but also the undesirable out-group attitudes. Hence the teacher needs to know the association between Socialization ability and attitudes. Then it is easy for the teacher to divide the class into groups especially for the project work.

The teacher will also be able to understand better the implication of following these activities, for example, change in Socialization ability leading to positive attitudes and better attitudes leading to high socialization ability.

It is of utmost importance to know this association in an adolescent, as adolescence is the transit period between child hood and adult hood. It is normally a difficult period for the social group as well as the individual. The structure of adolescent group is likely to be much more complex than that of groups of younger children. Usually, an adolescent wants to relieve his conflicts and tensions in the group especially in the peer group.

One of the importance purposes of education is to aid individuals to personal, social, and economic progress. The various agencies like school, home, mass media and peer group affect the individual.

In adolescent period these agencies have a greater influence, especially the peer group. Different degrees of social acceptance may have different effects of adolescent attitudes.

Adolescence is a period of psycho-social physical change. In later adolescence individuals become more stable. They are aware of the friendship choices and factors working for these relations.

In this period positive moral characterization also takes place. For this, an adolescent should have proper attitudes, and knowledge skills also, apart from other skills. So it is of utmost importance to know the friendship choices or who a popular, isolate or rejectee is. Through this we can understand the socialization ability of adolescents and ways to improve them. By knowing the association between socialization ability, the attitudes especially scientific attitudes and attitude towards science; it may be possible for the teacher to improve the socialization ability, develop scientific attitude and attitude towards science in a more planned manner.

FOCUS OF THE STUDY

The Junior College students are in the stage of late adolescence. They are in the age group of seventeen plus. These adolescent college students are at a crucial stage in their life. They possess all the characteristics of adolescents and are passing through the adolescent crisis.

They are in a process of developing moral character, developing different tastes, and interests. They have aspirations and attitudes.

These students have completed five years of primary schooling and five years of high school education. They received science education during all these ten years, both in primary and high school levels.

The students may also develop some general characteristics during this educational stage. Some of these characteristics are : (i) fulfilment of educational and vocational aspirations (ii) competitive spirit (iii) general tendency to study well to fulfil his ambitions. As to the psychological tendencies the student develop all the characteristics of an individual in the late adolescent stage. A personality of his own is built and he tries to be independent. He generally gets into association as is the characteristic of late adolescent and acquires peer group attitudes.

In Indian scenario, modernity and superstition live together. Despite the recent technological developments, the pupil may still be living in traditional culture. An adolescent child (junior college) is exposed to this type of environment. So he may automatically learn all traditions, customs and prejudices prevailing in the society.

The nature of science education and the way it is imbibed by the individual, can be influencing his attitude towards science and scientific attitude. Keeping the above aspects in view, the study proposes to focus its attention on knowing the nature of and relationship between socialization ability, scientific attitude and attitude towards science.

Further, the focus is on identifying the influence of the following variables : type of institution, medium of learning, class environment and discipline on the three dependent variables of the study. The following are the reasons for choosing these variables.

Because of the taboos and customs of the Indian society, there is a definite segregation between boys and girls. The girls are not given as much freedom as that of a boy, which may effect their socialization ability. Girls are also attributed with conservative tendencies, and at times are known to oppose changes. Hence this may be influencing their attitude towards science and scientific attitude. This is the reason why sex was chosen as a variable in this study.

While a majority of the junior colleges are non-residential, the recent tendencies in collegiate education at this level have evolved residential junior colleges. Most of these students, who have aspirations for better success in science education, are joining the residential colleges. Their ulterior motive is to succeed in the competitive race for joining professional courses like medicine and engineering. In residential system the students stay together, live together, sit together, eat together, work together, and, play together. This closeness may result in better group cohesiveness, better in group associations, and better socialization ability. Since these facilities are not available in non residential system, the two categories of students, namely, residential and non-residential may be differing with reference to Socialization ability. The competitive spirit, of the residential students, may be influencing their scientific attitude and attitude towards science leading to the differences between the residential and non-residential students, hence this variable was considered to be important for this study.

Learning through mother tongue enables one to understand, acquire, and interpret knowledge in a better manner. Science education through mother tongue may result in well understood scientific knowledge, better scientific attitude, and attitude towards science. But most of the students prefer English as medium of learning at collegiate level. Most and a good number of academically forward students also prefer English as a medium of learning. The investigator could not reason out who is going to be better in reference to scientific attitude and attitude towards science. Similarly the socioeconomic-backgrounds of Telugu medium students is generally different from English medium students; because of the other aspects like aspirations, achievement, which may lead to the selection of the medium of learning, there are chances for difference in socialization ability between Telugu medium and English medium students in junior colleges. Hence medium of learning was selected as another variable.

One of the factors that can influence peer group associations and socialization ability is the classroom. The class room can be co-educational. Some times the classroom may be of the uni-sex category comprising of either exclusively boys or exclusively girls. This may not be a variable, influencing socialization ability in western classroom environment, but even in the co-educational classroom, generally there is definite segregation and ganging into boys gangs and girls gangs. There is a possibility for different peer group structures in co-educational or uni-sex classrooms leading to differences in socialization ability. There are no reasons to believe that co-education or uni-sex classroom may influence the scientific attitude and attitudes towards science of Junior college students. Hence this variable, namely, 'class environment' is also included.

Science courses are preferred by those, who want to get into technical and science related professions. Studying science is comparatively more strenuous exercise than studying arts. Science students are knowledge oriented and arts students are social oriented. This may lead to difference in socialization ability between arts and science students. For the purpose of this study, though the sample is classified into arts and science students, this bifurcation and entry into science and art streams is just two years old as far as these post adolescent students are concerned. All of them had science education at school level. Hence there may not be a difference as far as scientific attitude and attitudes towards science are concerned. But this variable, namely, 'discipline' was felt important for this study because of its expected differences in socialization ability.

For the purpose of this the investigator has decided to make a study of socialization ability, scientific attitude and attitudes towards science among junior college students who are in late adolescence.

RESEARCH QUESTIONS

In order to make an investigation of the three traits, among college students and their nature of association the following research questions were framed.

1. How are the traits socialization ability, scientific attitude and attitudes towards science distributed in junior college students?
2. In the chosen population, is there any association between these traits?

TITLE OF THE STUDY

SOCIALIZATION ABILITY, SCIENTIFIC ATTITUDE AND ATTITUDES TOWARDS SCIENCE IN JUNIOR COLLEGE STUDENTS—A STUDY

OBJECTIVES OF THE STUDY

The following are the objectives framed.

1. To identify the trend of distribution of the socialization ability in junior college students?
2. To study the scientific attitude of junior college students.
3. To find out the attitude the students have towards science.
4. To study the association among the three traits, namely:

   (a) Socialization ability.
   (b) Scientific attitude.
   (c) Attitude towards science.

5. To study the variable wise association among the three traits namely:

   (a) Socialization ability.
   (b) Scientific attitude.
   (c) Attitude towards science.

6. To identify the influence of the following variables on socialization ability, scientific attitude and attitude towards science in junior college students.

   (a) Sex
   (b) Type of Institution
   (c) Medium of learning
   (d) Class environment
   (e) Discipline

In the forthcoming chapter the researcher made an attempt to review the related literature which facilitated the drawing of the design of the study and to determine the scope of the study.

2

Related Literature

For any worthwhile study in any field of knowledge, a research worker needs an adequate familiarity with the library and its many resources. Only then will an effective search for specialized knowledge be possible. The search for reference material is a time-consuming but very fruitful phase of a research programme. Every investigator must know what sources are available in his field of enquiry, which of them he is likely to use, and where and how to find them.

Hence, a brief review of the previous investigations pertaining to the present study is found to be very essential. Many studies have been carried out using the sociometric-technique in an attempt to analyse the nature of dynamic relationship among individuals forming groups. Sociometric devices have been utilized in improving the quality of social interactions. There are also studies made on scientific attitude and attitude towards science.

In this chapter, the studies which were conducted in India and abroad mainly to study the socialization ability of pupils in relation to different variables and studies on scientific attitude and attitude towards science are reported.

SOCIALIZATION ABILITY

1. Social Relationships

(a) *Cattell—Friends and Enemies*

Raymond B. Cattell (1934), studied 'Friends and enemies'—a psychological study of character and temperament. The method of study was the administration of Temperament Test II with an aim to study the 'General temperament' and 'General will characters'. The conclusions are: "The most popular persons will have moderately high surgency, very high will character and very low preservation. The most unpopular person will have high surgency, very low will character, and very high preservation.

(b) *Vreeland and Corey College Friendships*

A study of 'college friendships' was made by Francis M. Vreeland and Stephen M. Corey. Vreeland and Corey selected 5 psychological tests, namely, "Thurstone personality schedule", "Thurstone psychological examination for college students", "Drobas attitude towards war scale", "Moss social intelligence examination", and Watson's Test of Public Opinion on some religious and economic issues. The most important conclusions are: The part played by intelligence in the formation of friendship is said to be hazardous. The intimate friends are slightly superior in academic grades. The parents of friends are in same vocation, similar in their social intelligence. The neurotic personality has few friends of the opposite sex. Attitude towards peace is found to be an irrelevant factor in the selection of friends.

(c) *Richardson, Forester, Shukla and Higginbotham—Friendship*

Richardson *et al.* (University of Lcndon 1948-54) studied 'positive inter personal relations, i.e., friendship'. The method for investigation was the administration of a questionnaire, interviewing important cases and asking the subject to write an essay on 'My friend'. A list of twelve geographical projects was organised and subjects were allowed to group accordingly. The most important significant conclusion regarding friendship choices are: Selection of friends is related to the satisfaction of psychological needs. Both boys and girls tend to group on unisexual bases and the relationship with the opposite sex is unstable. The reciprocation on ten criteria is very significant. I.Q. is highly significant among girls. Boys merely mention 'physical appearance', in their essays on 'My Best Friend' whereas girls mention physical appearance along with other characteristics. There is beginning of hetero-sexual interest also, and the friendship serves mostly the growing need of children.

(d) *Austin and Thompson—Children's Friendships*

Mary C. Austin and George Thompson (1948) studied "children's friendships". Sociometric technique was used. It is concluded that the selection of friends depends on twenty-one heads which are positive in nature. The important variable in this study is found to be 'propinquity' as the basis for children's friendships.

(e) *Bonny—Friendship Choices in Colleges*

In 1949 M.E. Bonny studied 'friendship choices in college in relation to church affiliation in church, family size and length of enrolment in college'. He adopted both the techniques of the analysis—coliometric and psychological. The important and significant conclusions are: The students not aligned to any church receive friendship choices beyond choice expectancy. All the churches except Christian show in-group preferences. The student not belonging to any church show high degree in-group references.

(f) *Mayer—Seat Partner*

A study of Mayer, *et al.* (1949) in connection with choice of seat partner in the classroom showed that there was a slight tendency to choose a partner in relation to one's own colour (race) with positive factors in choice.

(g) *Kinney—Flexible Groups*

The study by Kinney, Elve E. (1950) suggested that children in the small flexible group tended to show improvement in social acceptance by their classmates.

(h) *Darley, Gross and Martin—Study of Group Behaviour*

John, G. Darley *et al.* (1950) carried out 'studies of group behaviour, stability, change, and inter-relations of psychometric and sociometric variables'. The method was further improved by collecting the psychometric, sociometric, and autobiographical data. The important and significant conclusions were: There was no selective and assertive grouping in all the thirteen houses on different factors. Though assertive at the beginning, by the end of the year in all the thirteen houses individual changes occurred in the direction of creating homogeneity of variance. Higher amounts of paired choices in certain sociometric choices and higher ratios of in-group to out-group choices by the end of the year were found to be related to the score on 'satisfaction with village life'.

(i) *Arthor—Aspects of Personality*

In a study by Singer Arthor (1951), a high degree of constancy was found in friendship choices and education aspects.

(j) *Dymond—Choosing Friends*

Dymond and her associates observed that 2nd grades were choosing friends on the basis of external qualities such as money and a nice home.

(k) *Sandrette—Social Distance and Degree of Acquaintance*

Onas C. Sandrette of Wheaton College, Wheaton (Illinois) (1958) studied 'Social distance and degree of acquaintance'. The 'acquaintanceship scale' and 'social distance scale' were used as testing measures. The main conclusion was that the stronger degree acquaintanceship will increase an individual's chances of being chosen as a friend, if he has socially acceptable personality traits.

(l) *Otto—Status of Pupil*

The study of Dahle H. Otto (1953) indicated that in sociometric choice, the evaluate system, most important for children appeared to be sex status first and secondary pupil status.

(m) *Buswell—School Work*

In a study by Buswell, Margaret M. (1953), it was concluded that when we considered a class room of boys and girls in either the early grades or the higher grades, it may be said in general those who are succeeding in school work will also be succeeding in their social relationship with their peers.

(n) *Gronlund—Stability*

In the study of Gronlund, Norman E. (1955) it was found that the first choice is the most stable one with a steady decrease in stability to the fifth choice. So in the present study three choices were taken giving differential weightage for each choice.

(o) *Richard—Self-perceptions*

According to Richard M. Lemdy (1958) the statements of relationships between self perceptions and descriptions of sociometric choices are of the same or opposite sex.

(p) *Landus—Intelligence*

In the study of Landus and others (1958), it was found that a boy's social power determines his behaviour more than his intelligence does.

(q) *Boyd and June—Play Companions*

In a study by Boyd, R. *et al.*, 'the choices of play companions by preschool children' were analysed. Children were found to prefer play companions of their own sex, this tendency being more pronounced in boys than in girls.

(r) *Mary, Commins, and Edward—The Complementarity of Personality Needs in Friendship Choice*

Mary, St. Anne Reilly, *et al.* (1959-60), made a study on 'the complementarity of personality needs in friendship choice'. The instruments used were (1) Edward personal—preference, schedule and (2) Allport Vernon study of values. The most significant conclusions were: Friends tend to be similar in values. There is no conclusive evidence of similarity of needs of friends and mutual needs satisfaction. There is no complementary relationship in regard to self perceiving personality.

2. Sociometric Choices

(a) *Grace—Gifted Children*

In a study of 294 children by Grace *et. al.*, on gifted children, it was concluded that the gifted child is not a social isolate within the first six grades of the urban school chosen for the study. The children with highest selection-rejection scores were more intelligent, had more reading ability, came from houses of higher status and had more personal adjustment.

(b) *Grossman—Selection-Rejection Scores*

Grossman *et al.* (1948) in their study found rejected children were on the whole more susceptible to nervous symptoms.

(c) *Endleman and Scholom-Group Structure*

In a study by Endleman and Scholom (1963) the main finding is that the tighter the group structure, the more freedom for the individual.

(d) *Epperson—Isolation of Children*

Epperson, D.C. (1963) studied 'The isolation of children' and found that neglecting of pupils is also one of the factors determining the isolation of children.

(e) *Deno—Social Status*

Deno, Stanley L. *et al.* (1981) from their study results indicated that observed peer to target child behaviour was related to the social status of the target child with low status being talked to less than either middle or high status.

3. Sociometric Status

(a) *Jennings—Leadership*

Jennings (1943) studied 'leadership'. A technique relating to sociometric technique by J.L. Moreno is used. Study of the reasons given for the sociometric choices and rejection led to the conclusion that leadership was not explainable by any particular personality characteristics or constellation of traits.

(b) *Bonney—Personality Adjustment*

A group of 50 children in an elementary school were studied by Bonney (1944) using the California test of personality and multiple-criterion sociometric questionnaire. He found that the total adjustment score of the inventory correlated 0.49 with sociometric status. It was also found that those who are high in social choice are also the highest in mean adjustment scores.

(c) *Northway—Personal Adjustment*

Northway (1944) has suggested that sociometric data provided evidence of the acceptance of the person within a specific social setting.

(d) *Kuhlen and Bretch—Personal Adjustment*

Kuhlen and Bretch (1947) compared the upper and lower quartiles in sociometric status of 692, ninth grade in their responses to 'Mooney—Problem check-list'. The findings indicated that those low in status tended to check a significantly larger number of problems as "often" present.

(e) *Northway and Widger—Personal Adjustment*

Northway and Widger (1947) have compared 'Rorschah responses' of three groups of eighth grade boys and girls who were high, low and middle in sociometric status. The authors indicated that those high in status were characterised by "greater sensitivity in sensing the feeling of others and consciously striving for the approval of others", the middle groups "seemed a more shallow, less introspective group, few anxiety or emotional disturbances". The low group seemed to be the most seriously disturbed. They showed less ability to control their emotions, and seem to be a more egocentric, moody, and impulsive group.

(f) *Grossman and Wrighter—Personal Adjustment*

Grossman and Wrighter (1948) found that sixth grade students who were very high in sociometric status secured much higher total adjustment scores on the California Test of personality than did a similar group of students who were very low in sociometric status.

(g) *French and Mensh—Personality Variables*

French and Mensh (1948) studied 34 college students who were members of the same sorority. A technique relating to 'sociometric technique' by J. L. Moreno is used. The most significant conclusion was that in general the individuals, high in choice status were rated highest on those personality variables that are normatively most valued.

(h) *Baron—Personal Adjustment*

Baron (1951) divided a larger number of fifth and sixth grade students into three sociometric status groups and compared in their response to a mental health inventory. Those groups who are low in social status make more "on favourable" responses than either of the other groups.

(i) *Cox—Personal Adjustment*

Cox (1953) obtained sociometric choices for 52 children (aged 5 to 13) in an Australian Orphanage. Sociometric status was found to correlate 0.76 with composite adjustment ratings based on TAT stories, a social adjustment questionnaire, and interviews with those caring for the children. Cox concluded that sociometric status was a sensitive and valued index of behavioural change.

(j) *Mills—Personal Adjustment*

The M.M.P.I. Rorschach and TAT were utilised by Mills (1953). It was found that in all the three measuring instruments, there is a consistent picture of contrasting adequacy of adjustment between the sociometrically popular and unpopular students.

(k) *Lindzey and Goldwys—Personality Variables*

Lindzey and Goldwys (1954) examined the relation between sociometric status, measured by choice and rejection, and certain PF study scores and TAT variables. The findings indicated that those high in sociometric status were less extrapernative, more intrapernative and showed lower groups conformity ratings than those of low in social status.

(1) *Marks—Personality Adjustment*

Marks (1954) administered an interest test and a sociometric questionnaire to 730 students in grades 8 to 12. In general the acceptable adolescent is seen as sociable, involved with people, and relatively impulsive.

(m) *Croft and Grygier—Personal Adjustment*

Croft and Grygier (1956) gave a sociometric test to 13 classes of eleven-to fifteen year olds in a secondary school in a poor neighbourhood. It was found that sociometric status was negatively related to teacher ratings of 'bad classroom behaviour'. It was also found that truant and delinquent boys had lowered sociometric status than the other students.

(n) *Semler—Personal Adjustment*

Semler (1960) found substantial positive correlation between sociometric status and personal adjustment as measured by teacher ratings and the California test of personality.

1. Sociometric Status and Friendship Choices

(a) *Chowdhari—Friendship*

K.P. Chowdhari (1952) studied 'linguistic groupings' in Delhi Multilingual Schools. The subjects were asked to choose 30 friends from among his or her school fellows in 10 different situations (3 in each). There was no bar in choosing the same friends for different situations. It was concluded that the disintegrated group tried to cling to the group with highest social status. Large group alien to the culture of the religion and other large groups not enjoying high status were worst placed for inter linguistic friendship. The factors given below were expected to have liberalising influence on inter-group friendships. (a) Participation on out-door sports, (b) Visit to out side states, (c) Friendship with people outside India, (d) Extent of news paper and journal reading, and (e) Marriage of Intimate relations to people speaking a different language.

(b) *Sudha—Paired Friendship*

Sudha Malhotra (1969) studied 'the aspect of interpersonal relationship—the relationship between two's'. The main aim of the work was to investigate the factors underlying the pairing of friends during later-adolescence. An 'interest inventor', 'Jalota group intelligence test', 'TAT', a 'sentence completion test' were taken as tools. The following are the main conclusions: Paired friends are similar in (a) socio economic status (b) language (c) culture (d) land (e) living habits. They are affected by proximity, are attracted by behaviour patterns, and in case of girls attracted by studied and intellectual qualities, by assertive qualities, and similar in trends of sentiments and similar in anxiety state.

2. Sociometric Status

(a) *Shakuntala*

In 1954 Shakuntala Bhalla worked on 'sociometry in the classroom'. Sociometric test was conducted. The significant findings were the childrens' interrelations ran counter to those of the teacher aided organisation of groups. Segregation of sexes were preferred.

(b) *Sharma*

Sharma (1970) made a 'sociometric study'. A technique similar to 'sociometric technique' by J.L. Moreno is used. The study showed that out of 1213 students in 36 Delhi schools, about two-thirds of the students in each class were "unaccepted" for any of these three activities. According to Sharma, the percentage of neglectees and of isolates in this study is much more than in studies in other countries. Sharma reports that the populars were on the average, of higher intelligence and adjustment scores than isolates and scored high in scholastic achievement also. The fathers of populars had high income and education than the fathers of isolates. It was also found that popular were more aggressive, assertive, vigorous, confident, and friendly than the unaccepted students.

(c) *Pathak—Adjustment Level*

Pathak (1971) studied 'The sociometric status and adjustment level in school children'. Data were collected through 'Vyaktika Paraka Prashnvali' 'adjustment inventory', 'teachers rating scale' and percentage of school marks in two consecutive years. Pathak (1971) found that the populars were significantly superior to all the other three groups in home adjustment, social adjustment and emotional adjustment. The rejectees and the isolates were comparable in name, social, emotional, and school adjustments, but they differed in health adjustments and rejectees were inferior to the isolates in scholastic achievement and personality dimension. Finally he concludes that sociometric status is being significantly related to the various grades of adjustment.

(d) *Bajpeyi—Intelligence*

Bajpeyi (1971) studied 'The sociometric status of high school students and its relation to intelligence and interest pattern'. His tools were 'general mental ability' (Joshi), 'interest pattern'

(Singh), 'sociometric questionnaire', and 'socio-economic status scale' (Urban). The most important results made were: There was significant difference in mechanical area of interest. The popular boys and girls have significantly greater interest in scientific and social fields. Populars had significantly higher socio economic status than the neglectees and rejectees.

(c) *Nagar—Personality Characteristics*

Nagar (1973) made 'A comparative study on personality characteristics of socially accepted and rejected girls of higher secondary schools of Agra city'. The significant results were: On the whole socially accepted students tended to make higher academic achievement in comparison of socially unaccepted students. Stars tended to be more rational and thoughtful than the rejectees.

(f) *Upamanyu—Scholastic Attainment*

'A investigation in to the relationship between sociometric status and scholastic achievement' was made by Vishwa Vijay Upamanyu (1973). Sociometric technique developed by Morena was used in order to know the sociometric status of the students. The scholastic achievement of populars was significantly higher as compared to isolates and rejectees.

(g) *Upamanyu—Different Components of Anxiety*

Upamanyu (1974) studied 'The relationship between sociometric status and different components of anxiety'. The tools used were, the sociometric technique developed by Moreno, and IPAT anxiety scale questionnaire. His major findings are: Anxiety and sociometric status were negatively correlated. Isolates and rejectees did not differ in their anxiety level. Ego weakness was found to be an important factor for the isolation or rejection of subjects. Rejectees scored maximum on this component.

3. *Joshi—Study of the Star and Isolate Girls*

Joshi (1980) has made 'A sociometric study of star and isolate girls'. The stars differed from the isolates in certain personal and psychological factors. Among the environmental factors the nearest friends of the stars had a high achievement level, had very little outside help for studies, and belonged to higher Income families.

(a) *Sharma—Correlates of Sociometric Status*

Sharma (1974) had taken up 'The correlates of sociometric status in high school classes'. The researcher used Vyaktika Parakha Prashnavalli, interest inventory, and a questionnaire. The significant results are: Intelligence played an important role in making the students accepted in the group. The least liked skills and activities for both the groups were indoor games, religious activities, and mechanical work.

(b) *Patel—Sociometric Variables*

Patel (1975) investigated 'The sociometric variables and their correlates'. The tools used were (i) sociometric test (ii) The Marill-Palmer personality rating schedule; (iii) The seven point scale (iv) the Minnesota personal scale (v) The Brides scale of social development. He found that there was no relationship between opportunity for contact with classmates and sociometric status and between age and sociometric status.

(c) *Misra—Personality Traits*

Misra (1981) studied 'The relationship between personality traits and sociometric choices in classroom'. The tools used were adjustment inventory for school students (Sinha and Singh), sociometric questionnaire, and personality trait preference scale. The most important findings of the study were: A person with four choices on the average enjoyed leadership. Adjusted subject chose and reciprocated with adjusted counterparts. Co-efficient of correlation between self-rating and rating about friend on personality characteristics appeared to be significant.

(d) *Chauhan—Self Concept*

Chauhan (1982) studied 'The sociometric correlates of self concept'. The tools used were 'Atmapodhi .Mapini and Semantic differential scales'. The main finding of the study were: There was no difference among the three dimensions of sociometric structure. There was no relationship between the factors of self concept and the dimensions of sociometric structure.

(e) *Madhosh—Personality*

Madhosh (1982) studied the personality correlates of sociometric status in different interpersonal situations. The tools used were 'Cattels 16 P.F. inventory', and Sociometric test. The most important finding of the studies are: The most desirable personality traits among the students of Jammu and Kashmir region were outgoing socially, bold, and relaxed but those from the Ladakh region were shy and conservative. (ii) The populars of Jammu Kashmir region were intelligent, outgoing, warm hearted, socialiy bold, and relaxed, but those of Ladakh region were just the contrast.

A study was also made to find out the socio-psychological characteristics of sociometric star and social isolates (1985). The main findings of the study were (1) The mean adjustment scores for sociometric stars were high in all the five areas (2) There was a positive relationship between levels of intelligence, socio-economic status, and achievement with social acceptability.

Personality profiles of socially rejected and their academic performance were also made (1986). The major conclusions were (1) The rejectees had a specific personality profile characterised by a set of traits but the degree of rejection did not vary with the degree of traits and academic performance, even though the academic performance of rejectees was poor.

D.S. Sripada Swamy conducted a study on the dynamic relationships among IX standard students of D.M.S. of Mysore which is a coeducation school. The major conclusions were (1) The choice of students chosen as leaders was directly influenced by superior achievement in curricular and co-curricular activities, and by personal quality. Dr. Aparajita Chowdhury *et al.*, (1997) made a study on 'Sociometric status and development of self concept in elementary school children'. 'The peer nomination sociometric test of Cole, Dodge, and Coppotelli' (1982) was used which had the procedures to classify the children into different sociometric status with respect to age and class, etc., in the class room situations. The study revealed that boys were rejected by their peers in greater numbers than their counterpart girls during late childhood. Moreover, it was found out that, there exists a marginal difference in different areas of self-concepts between the elementary schools boys and girls belonging to different sociometric status. Parents of popular children were found to give more opportunity to their children to have outside visits at least once in a week, whereas such type of exposure was found to be less frequent among peer rejected children. About fifty (50 %) per cent of the popular children were found to spend at least 3 to 4 hours per day with their peers whereas only fifteen per cent (15 %) of peer rejected children spent their time in peer group activities. Though not much significant difference was obtained in the development of self-concept among subjects belonging to different sociometric status groups, the trend for the popular group was certainly towards the development of positive self concept.

Though not a direct study on sociometric status another "study of some factors and processes involved in the development of values" was done by Roy, B.K. The major finding was the standard of adolescent values was lower than expected, and development of values was lower than expected, and development of value system was positively related with the process of socialization. The other major findings are: (1) Values are developed with the advancement of age and grade. (2) In the development of values the influential process of socialization were rationalization and appreciation, mutation, identification, and suggestion came next, and the process of alienation had no significant relation with grade/age (3) Boys and girls differ in their values but not in the process of socialization (4) Social intelligence has significant positive relation with devotion.

Tools and Techniques Used to Measure Socialization Ability

Sociometric Methods

There are four methods of measuring social relations in general.

A. Choice criteria

1. Sociometric matrix

2. Sociogram

In sociometric matrix the sociometric test results are summarised in a matrix table which is an NXN set of rows and columns. N is the number of subjects constituting the group taking the sociometric test, the rows represent the persons who make a choice or rejection, a column represents the persons chosen, unchosen, or rejected. Names of the persons must be arranged in the same order on both the axes. By giving the negative weightages of the rejection, the total number of choices received by each individual are added and on the basis of this sociometric status is calculated. Finally, according to their sociometric status peoples are classified as populars, isolates, rejectees, and neglectees as per the scores obtained.

Sociogram is a diagrammatic summary of the results of sociometric test. It consists of lines and arrows. The choice is represented by bold lines, the rejection by broken lines, and the arrow indicates the direction of the choice or rejection. The relative distances in the location of the individual members of the group express the extent of attraction or repulsion.

B. Sociometric Questionnaires

The questionnaire was used to measure the Socialization ability of the students.

C. Socio-empathy

Socio-empathy is a measure by which each individual can accurately estimate which other members in the tested group would choose him on a particular criterion listed.

D: Measure of Reputation

1. Guess who technique
2. The social distance scale

Guess who technique is used to obtain individual's opinions of one another with regard to number of traits. A spontaneous response is needed here.

Social distance scale attempts to measure to what degree an individual or a group of individuals is accepted, or rejected by another individual or a group. Various selected situations ranging from acceptance to rejection are established. The individual checks his position by choosing one of the points on the scale.

Tools Used in Various Studies

Sociometric techniques was used by Mary C. Austin, George Thompson, T.L. Green, Jennings, Bonny, French and Mensch, French, Lemaunn and Salmon, Lindzey Urban, Marks, Croft and Grygier, K.P. Chowdhari, Sudha Malhotra, Shakuntala Bhalla, Sharma, Bajpayi, Vishaw Vijay Upamanyu, Upamanyu Joshi, Sharma, Patel, Misha, Madhosh, Daljit Indra Singh, Kumari Sudha, Jamed S.K., Dhondiyal N.C., S.L. Chopra, Kaur, D., Say, A., Salodkar M.P., S. Jaya Kumari, Aparajita Chowdhari, *et al.*, Navare Savita Raghunath, Desouza, and D.S. Sripada Swamy.

Though not mentioned in any of the studies, On friendship choices, seat partner, flexible group or group's behaviour, friendship choices in relation to other variables sociometric technique is used by Raymond B. Cattell, Francis M. Vreeland and Stephen M. Corey, Richardson *et al.*, Bonny, Mayer, Kinney, John G. Darly, *et al.*, L., Arthor S., Dymond, Otto D.H., Buswell, Margaret M., Gronlund, Norman E., Richard M.L., C. Landus, Boyd R. *et al.*, Mary St. Anne Reilly, *et al.*, Grace., Grossman *et al.*, Endleman and Scholam, Eperson, Deno Stanley. L. *et al.*, Northway, Kuhlen and Bretch, Northway and Widger, Grossman and Wrighter, Baron, Fuller and Baune, Tigiury, Cox, Mills, Lindzey and Goldwys, Dunningtion, Davids and Parenti, Semler, Pathak, Nagar, Chaulin, Social distance scale is used by Onas C. Sandrette and T.L. Green.

Even though the researcher has used sociometric technique as in the previous studies reported, the present study is important as it is related to attitude towards science and scientific attitude as there is not a single study relating these studies.

SCIENTIFIC ATTITUDE

1. Caldwell and Lundeen

O.W. Caldwell and Gerhard E. Lundeen made a study on

'Student Attitudes regarding unfounded beliefs'. They found that high school seniors believed in slightly more than 20 per cent of a list of superstitions. The high school seniors were apparently affected by about 22 per cent of the superstitious ideas with which they were familiar.

2. Davis

Ira C. Davis. (1935) measured 'scientific attitudes' and found that the high school pupils in Wisconsin were not superstitious. The high school pupils of Wisconsin seemed to have a fairly clear concept of the cause and effect relationship, but they did not seem to be able to recognize the adequacy of a supposed cause to produce the given result.

3. Downing

Elliot, R. Downing studied 'Some results of a test on scientific thinking'. While testing the established conclusion, i.e., 'any increased power in critical thought processes or in scientific attitudes develops independently of, or possibly despite, science instruction', found that there was a fairly uniform and gradual increase in abilities from grade, viz., 2500 pupils in grades 8 through 12. He also found that the students who had not studied science scored average and high scores on the test of the scientific thinking than those who studied science. There was no evidence that science subjects, as they are conveniently taught, have higher powers of scientific thinking.

4. Noll

Noll, V.H. measured the 'scientific attitude' by devising a test. It focused on the following characteristics: Accuracy in opinions, intellectual honesty, open mindedness, suspended judgement, looking for true cause and effect relationship, and criticalness.

5. Kerkeurst

Arthur, J. Kerkeurst made a study on 'the acceptance of superstitious beliefs among secondary school pupils'. He found that the college degree students were not free from superstitions. Belief in superstitions does not decline with the advancement in grade levels despite the fact that the majority of the 500 pupils belonging to 7th, 8th and 9th grades were presumably taking or had taken science courses.

6. Alpern

Morris, L. Alpern undertook a study to find out the relationship between choice of science course a student has made and an ability to test hypotheses. He reported that there is no significant relation between the science courses a student had taken and his ability to select sound procedures to test hypotheses. The high school students have not developed the skill as a result of their instruction.

7. Baumel and Berger

Howard B. Baumel and J. Joel Berger made an attempt to measure scientific attitudes'. The purpose of the test was (1) to measure student ability to distinguish between scientifically determined facts and commonly half beliefs (2) To test student ability in evaluating experimental situations in terms of evidence available for valid conclusions. (3) To test student ability to formulate conclusions based upon sufficient evidence. (4) To measure student ability to suspend judgement in non experimental situations.

The results revealed that (a) Students who scored high were not necessarily those with grades in science and (b) Students who scored low were not necessarily those with low grades in science.

Baumel and Berger also hypothesise that the scientific attitudes may be developed with the help of the following factors (1) Scientifical attitudes may be acquired by students at all ability. (2) The science teacher needs to evaluate not only the knowledge achievement of the students, but also their growth in scientific attitude. (3) The student with scientific attitude will more effectively cope with problems in school and community. (4) Success in developing Scientific attitude depends ultimately on the teacher. The teacher through his actions must be able to convince the students that scientific attitude is an integral part of his behaviour. His intellectual honesty, willingness to admit error, listening to other ideas, dealing with facts in an unbiased way and make a favourable and a lasting impressions on pupils.

8. Kulkarni

B.G. Kulkarni made an 'An investigation into attitude of pupils, parents, and teachers towards work experience'. He found that the work experience was effective in inculcating in the pupils love of scientific attitude.

9. Shrivastava

'A study of the scientific attitude and its measurement' was done by N.N. Shrivastava. He found that science teachers and non science teachers, sciences students and non science students demonstrated positive scientific attitudes. The knowledge of science or general exposure to science courses affected the scientific attitude positively. He also found that scientific knowledge helped in the formation of scientific attitude. He also observed that scientific attitude differed in respect of sex in early ages, No significant difference in male and female teacher's scientific attitude is revealed and this was due to advancement in age. Shrivastava also revealed that the amount of scientific knowledge or general exposure to science courses had impact on scientific attitude positively, and scientific knowledge helped in the formation of scientific attitudes.

10. Ravindranath

M.J. Ravindranath made an experimental study on 'Development of Scientific attitude'. The main conclusion was that there was development of scientific attitude in both controlled and experimental pupils of VII class over a period of one academic year. The experimental group has developed scientific attitude to a considerable degree in comparison with the controlled group.

11. Bhaskara Rao, Sundara Rao and Mohana Rao

D. Bhaskara Rao *et al.*, made a study on 'Scientific attitude of experienced science teachers at secondary school level'. This study indicates that the quality of scientific attitudes held by this sample of science teachers is very poor. 65 per cent of the sample hold low scientific attitudes, only 35 per cent of them hold average scientific attitudes and unfortunately no one was with high scientific attitudes. The gradually decreased scientific attitudes were suspended judgement, respect for evidence, critical mindedness, honesty, and open mindedness.

12. Bhaskara Rao, Sundara Rao, Mohana Rao

D. Bhaskara Rao *et al.*, made a study on 'Scientific attitudes and personality traits of prospective science teachers'. They found that the prospective science teachers were also holding low scientific attitudes. The only scientific attitude that was predominant in experienced science teachers was willingness to change opinion to a great extent. Location (Rural/Urban) did not effect the possession of scientific attitude.

13. Bhaskara Rao, Sundara Rao, Aruna and Rathaiah

D. Bhaskara Rao *et al.*, made a study on scientific attitudes and personality traits of prospective science teachers with high pedagogic aptitude'. The trend of the data indicated that high pedagogic aptitude is related to the personality traits, radicalism and dominance. But, the low scientific attitude trend in prospective science teachers points out the need for curricular change in B.Ed. course and in-service training programmes. The use of composite criteria as admission requirement into teacher education, use of pedagogic aptitude measure, past scholastic achievement and competition scholastic measures are proposed.

14. Gopalakrishna

D. Gopalakrishna made 'A study of scientific attitude and its relation to intelligence of graduate students'. According to him the graduate students who were completely devoted to the science subject only have Scientific attitude. So far as specialization was concerned, the students of Zoology, Botany, Chemistry had definite advantage over the other students regarding the development of scientific attitude. He concluded that scientific attitude is not the sole monopoly of science subjects, but is equally capable of being developed among students of non-science subjects also. He also concluded that college degree students were not free from superstitions. Another important finding was that location, rural or urban did not influence the possession of scientific attitude.

15. Bhaskara Rao, Joseph Raju and Sundara Rao

D. Bhaskara Rao *et al.*, made a study on 'Scientific attitude of in-service and pre-service teachers'. The main finding is that the distribution of scientific attitudes under study is not normal and are distributed independently in the sample, and are independent of each other with out showing any relationship. In-service teachers exhibited a little higher degree of these attitudes. This study indicates that even science teachers, after having a long period of science education are not possessing scientific attitudes. This study points the need for developing systematic teacher training and in-service training programmes giving stress to scientific attitude.

16. Sood and Sanadhya

Scientific attitude scale was standardized by J.K. Sood and R. P. Sanadhya. The Scientific attitude scale consists of six dimensions based on the instrument developed by Billech and Zakharidas (1975), which consisted of six dimensions, viz., rationality, open mindedness, curiosity, aversion to superstition, objectivity of intellectual beliefs, and suspended judgement.

17. Bhaskara Rao

Bhaskara Rao made "A comparative study of scientific attitude, science aptitude, and achievement in biological science in secondary schools". A standardized scientific attitude scale by J.K. Sood and R.P. Sanadhya has used. The main conclusions with regard to scientific attitude are: The scientific attitude in secondary school pupils is average. The scientific attitude of pupils in all the subsample is average. The pupils studying in private schools, rural schools, English medium schools and non residential schools hold relatively better scientific attitude.

18. Curtis

Studies of Curtis, Blair and Goodson, and Vicklaund seem to show that direct teaching does modify the attitudes of young people and the study made by curtis gave rather clear evidence that pupils who engage in wide reading in general science develop scientific attitude more than those who study only single subject.

19. Klausmeirer

To develop attitudes, Klausmeirer suggests eight steps that the teachers can take to facilitate the learning of attitudes. A study on scientific attitudes and cognitive styles of higher secondary students was done in 1984. Some of the major finding are (1) about 80 per cent of the students had a positive scientific attitude. (2) Boys and girls did not differ in scientific attitude scores. (3) The scientific attitude of science students was higher than that of the arts and commerce students. (4) The rural students were found to have a low level of scientific attitude as compared to urban students. (5) The scientific attitude is significantly decreased with age.

ATTITUDE TOWARDS SCIENCE

1. Schebeci

R.A. Schebici (1986) made a study on 'Influence of students background and perceptions on science attitude and achievement'. The purpose of the study was to investigate the influence of student back ground and perceptions on science attitude and achievement. The main conclusions are: Sex, race and home environment were shown to have substantial influence on students achievement in science. Further two different models were tested: a model in which attitudes influence achievement and its converse. The data supported the first model, i.e., attitudes influencing achievement.

2. Pillai

Kamala S. Pillai (1987) made a study on 'Interactive effect of science aptitude and attitude towards science on biology achievement'. The results indicate that though there exists differences in biology achievement among secondary school pupils of three levels of science aptitude and three levels of attitude towards science, more significant interaction effect of science aptitude and attitude towards science on biology achievement exists.

3. Barrington and Handricks

Byson L. Barrington and Byson Handricks (1988) made a study on 'Attitude towards science and science knowledge of intellectually gifted and intellectually average grade students'. The important findings are: There was a significant difference between average and gifted students in attitudes towards being a scientist, usefulness of science and as might be expected in knowledge of science. Similarly there were significant difference between grades on attitude towards teacher and attitude towards science classes. There also was a significant interaction between grade level and ability regarding attitude towards science classes. Gender as a separate variable did not have a mean effect in any of the comparisons.

4. German

Paul J. German (1988) made a study on 'Development of attitudes towards science in school, assessment and its use to investigate the relationship, between the science achievement and attitude towards science in school'. A low correlation was found between attitude and various achievement tests. A moderate correlation was found between attitude and achievement that included an evaluation of the quality of works as in a course grade.

5. Cherylmason

Cherylmason (1988) studied 'Student's attitudes towards science and science related careers'. A programme designed to promote a stimulating gender free learning environment. The results indicated that the experimental group, compared to the control group, had significantly higher mean scores on the tests of attitude towards science, perception of science, extracurricular activities and interest in a science related career.

6. Steve

J. Steve, Oliver (1988) studied 'Influences of attitude towards science, achievement motivation, and science self concept, on achievement in science' which is a longitudinal study. This study has demonstrated that effective science behaviours in the science classrooms are strangely related to achievement. Although attitude toward science was not usually a powerful predication of achievement, in multiple regression equations, achievement motivation and science self concept were. Another important finding was, mathematics achievement did relate strongly to science self-concept. The attitude towards science subscale, and the science self concept sub scale were significant sources of variation with regard to this science mathematics differences. Based on the results of the study, there can be increased hope that changing attitudes will result in improved science achievement of particular importance is the contrast of self concept. Science self concept encourages students to achieve at a higher level in science.

7. Kelly

Kelly (1988) conducted a longitudinal study of 'students attitude towards science between ages of 11 and 13 paying particular attention to variation by sex and social class'. Student's attitudes in most areas of science declined over the 2 year period of time with the notable exceptions. Both males and females became more interested in finding more about human biology students. Opinions about science and scientists became more generally unfavourable but they became more willing to view science as suitable for females.

8. Unkikorn

T. Unkikorn (1988) investigated 'Attitudes towards science and achievement' among 709 students in VII, VIII, IX grades, in science class room in Thailand. The findings reveal that males possessed significantly more positive attitude towards science, there were no grade level difference; males attitudes towards science increase with years of schooling, whereas female attitudes decline with schooling. There was a significant difference in physical science achievement in grade 9, but not in 7th or 8th grades with males performing better. A significant difference in biology in grade '7' was noted with females scoring better.

9. Harty, Samuel and Beall

Harty, Samuel and Beall (1988) examined 'The relationship among the constructs of attitude towards science, interest in science, curiosity and self concept of science ability'. The results indicate that the attitude towards science, interest in science, and science curiosity are highly correlated.

10. Tatton and Simpson

Tatton and Simpson (1988) examined 'The relationship between self, home, classroom environment, and attitude towards science'. They found that classroom environment is under direct control of the educator and is significant.

Corol, Wareeng (1991) made 'A survey of antecedents of attitude towards science'. Results indicate a significant correspondence between report card grades, degree of structure, degree of stress, gender, degree of reward, number of tests, and students attitudes towards science.

11. Misti, et al.

Frank, L. Misti. Jr. *et al.*, (1991) prepared 'A science attitude scale for middle school students'.

12. German

Paul J. German (1995) tested 'A model of science process skills acquisition'. An interaction with parents education, preferred language, gender, science attitude, cognitive development, academic ability and biology knowledge. The important conclusions were : Each student variable was found to have significant effects accounting for approximately 80 per cent. Of the variance in science process skill achievement, academic ability, biology knowledge, and language preference has significant direct effects. There were significant mediated effects by cognitive development, parents education, and attitude towards science in school. The variables of cognitive development and academic ability had the greatest total effects on science process skills.

13. Dorothy, Peter and Judy

Dorothy, L. Gabel, Peter, A. Rubba and Judy, R. Franz made a study on 'The effect of early training and training experience on physics achievement, attitude towards science, and science teaching, and process skill proficiency'. Results of this study indicate that having students observe and teach in local elementary class rooms and placing increased emphasis on the science process skills, in the laboratory portion of their physics course had beneficial results. Both treatments appear to have significant effect on physics achievement.

14.. Bandyopadhay

Bandyopadhay, J. (1984) made a study of 'Environmental influence, academic achievement, and science aptitude as determinants of adolescent attitude towards science stream'. The major findings of the study are pupils having a high positive attitude towards science were different with respect to the independent variables either in isolation or interaction. The obtained casual factors were environmental, attitudinal and achievement related parental education, and SES led to favourable attitude towards science. Influences of teachers and peers, vocational value of science, future aim of life were other contributory factors. The pupils with high attitude towards comprehensive science possessed higher mechanical comprehensive and visualisation of objects in space.

15. Sudhir and Darehhingper

M.A. Sudhir and Darehhingper (1987) made 'A study on science achievement and science attitude among college students'. The results reveal significant sex differences in science achievement and attitude towards science among college students. Age and parental education inversely related to students achievement in science. Students from rural background and last born were found to be superior to the urban and the first and middle born in science achievement.

General Availability of Tools to Measure Attitude Towards Science and Scientific Attitude

From the studies mentioned above it is understood that the following tools and technique are available to measure attitude towards science.

1. Casual model procedure
2. Attitude of sub scales and content knowledge sub scales.
3. Attitude Towards Science in School Assessment (ATSSA).
4. Teacher intervention programme.
5. Science self concept sub scale. Attitude towards science sub scale.
6. Wareeng Attitudes Towards Science (WASP).
7. Likert type instrument (to assess attitude towards science).
8. A model of science process skill acquisition.
9. Simson—Troost attitude instrument.
10. "What is your Attitude towards science and science teaching by R.W. Moore", "The science process measure for teacher" developed by AAAS.
11. Likert scale attitude-modification science attitude scale for middle school students by Frank and Misti Jr.
12. Science Attitude Scale by Mrs. Avinash Grewal.

Through the review it was possible to identify the following tools and techniques used to measure scientific attitude.

1. Scientific attitude scale by Noll.
2. Test on understanding science (TOUS)
3. Allen's scale
4. Projective test of attitude by Lowery.
5. Science support scale by Schwirian.

6. An inventory of Scientific attitude by Moore and Sutman.
7. Scientific attitude measurement by Curtis.
8. The Scientific Attitude Scale (SAS) by Victory Biush and George A Lakhariades.
9. Scientific Attitude Scale by N.N. Shrivastava.
10. Scientific Attitude Scale by J. K. Sood and R.P. Sanadhya.
11. Scientific Attitude Test by M.J. Ravindranath.
12. Scientific Attitude Scale by D. Gopala Krishna.
13. Scientific Attitude Scale by M. James Kozlow and Marshall A. Nay.

From the above it can be seen there are various tools and techniques to measure attitude towards science and scientific attitude. But the investigator has used Scientific Attitude Scale by Mrs. Avinash Grewal and Scientific Attitude Scale developed by J.K. Sood and R.P. Sanadhya as they were found more suitable for present study.

From the above research studies it is evident there is not a single study relating socialization ability, attitude towards science and scientific attitude. Even though there are a few studies in which socialization ability was studied in correlation to many other variables, it is important that a study is made relating socialization ability to attitudes towards science and scientific attitude. The importance of a proper attitude towards science and scientific attitudes is already dealt in the previous chapter.

RELEVANCE OF THE STUDY

A number of studies are made (both abroad and in India), relating socio metric choice (sociometric status) with personal adjustment and found direct relationship between them. Various studied relating sociometric status and personality variables found a positive relationship between them. A few studies are made relating small flexible groups, group structures, group disintegration (linguistic group) to sociometric status. Sociometric status is also related to some psychometric and sociometric variables, aspects of personality and education, personality traits, personality correlates needs, personality characteristics and found a positive relation.

Few studies were also made relating sociometric status with sex status and pupils status, money and nice home, stability of choice, play companion of their own sex, common background, perceptions of friends, sports activities, age, caste, religion, and language and found a positive relation between them.

A positive relation was also found between sociometric status and achievement. Studies on self concept and sociometric status showed a positive relation between them. Some studies were also made relating sociometric status with maladjustment, accident proneness, behavioural change, intellectual and assertive qualities, sentiments, anxiety segregation, sex, length of residence, choice of workmate, and leadership traits.

Only two studies were made relating sociometric status with attitudes, that too peace attitudes and attitude towards church affiliation. As far as the researcher's knowledge goes there is not even a single study relating sociometric status with opinions towards knowledge, i.e., Attitude towards science, and scientific attitude which are important aspects in the present modernized society. Hence the researcher felt the need to study this untouched area of educational research in India.

Even though the tools and procedures followed are more or less similar to those already mentioned in previous studies, the present study becomes important, in that, it extends itself to an investigation of socialization ability of post adolescent students in relation to their scientific attitude and Attitude towards science.

The methods of investigation, design of the study, selection of tools or techniques and sampling are described in the next chapter.

3

Method of Investigation

This study of "Socialization ability, Scientific attitude, and Attitude towards science of Junior College Students" was undertaken to find out how these traits are distributed and to know whether there is any association between these traits.

The following objectives of the study were framed.

1. To identify the trend of distribution of the socialization ability in junior college students.
2. To find out the attitude the students have towards science.
3. To find the scientific attitude of junior college students.
4. To study the association among the three traits in junior college students, namely.

   (a) Socialization ability
   (b) Scientific attitude
   (c) Attitude towards science

5. To study the variablewise association among the three traits, namely.

   (a) Socialization ability
   (b) Scientific attitude
   (c) Attitude towards science

6. To identify the influence of the following variables on socialization ability, scientific attitude, and attitude towards science in junior college students.

   (a) Sex
   (b) Type of Institution
   (c) Medium of learning
   (d) Class environment
   (e) Discipline

A review of related studies and literature enabled the investigator to choose the method for conducting this study. Since this investigation comes under descriptive category of study, it was felt that 'Survey method' will help in gathering the data needed to answer the research questions.

RESEARCH DESIGN

The research design of the study is depicted in Table 3.1.

HYPOTHESES

I. The traits socialization ability, scientific attitude, and attitude towards science will be distributed normally in the sample of junior college students.
II. The traits socialization ability, scientific attitude, and attitude towards science will be associated with each other in the sample.
III. In all the sub-samples of junior college students there will be association between the three traits socialization ability, scientific attitude, and attitude towards science.
IV. The variables selected for the study, namely, sex, class environment, medium of learning, type of institution, and discipline will be the influencing variables of the three traits socialization ability, scientific attitude, and attitude towards science.

SELECTION OF TOOLS

As already pointed out, the traits to be measured from the

Table 3.1: *Socialization ability, scientific attitude and attitude towards science in Junior College Students*

S. No.	*Traits Measured*	*Tools*	*Source of data*	*Analysis of the Data*	*Variables of the study*
I.	Traits:				
1.	Socialization ability distribution	Socio Metric Technique By J.L. Moreno	Senior Intermediate Students	(a) Classification of socialisation ability (b) Verification of distribution trends with chisquare test (Normal distribution hypothesis)	
2.	Level of Scientific attitude	Scientific attitude scale by J. Sood and R.P. Sandhya	- do -	(a) Classification of level of Scientific attitude and Attitude towards science (b) Verification of normal distribution of hypotheses with chisquare test	
3.	Attitude Towards Science	Science attitude scale by Mrs. Avinash Grewal	- do -		

II.	Association of Traits				
	(a) Whole Sample (1-2; 2-3; 3-1)	–	- do -	(a) Contingency tables (b) Tests of independence	
III.	(b) Variablewise (1-2; 2-3; 3-1)	–	- do -		1. Sex 2. Class Environment 3. Medium of Learning 4. Type of Institution 5. Discipline
IV.	Influence of the variables on the three traits (1, 2,. 3)	–	- do -	(a) t-test	

sample are socialization ability, scientific attitude, and attitude towards science. While the latter two can be measured by using paper and pencil tools, i.e., attitude scales, the measurement of socialization ability has to be undertaken by using 'sociometric technique'. The tools selected for the study are described below.

SOCIALIZATION ABILITY TOOL

Sociometric questionnaire was used to find out the socialization ability of the students.

The researcher devised the sociometric questionnaire on the basis of the guidelines and the sample items given by J.L. Moreno (1939). It consists of four questions having three choices for each question. The questions were based on the two aspects.

(a) The group of pupils who like one another.

(b) The group of pupils who reject one another.

The following are the questions framed.

I. Whom do you like to sit with in your class ?

1.

2.

3.

II. Whom do you like to eat with during the lunch time ?

1.

2.

3.

III. Whom do you like to work with among your classmates in your college ?

1.

2.

3.

IV. Whom you do not like among your classmates ?

1.

2.

3.

To find out the socialization ability of the sample of junior college students, sociomatrices are drawn for each section separately. From the sociomatrices, pupil's sociometric scores were noted.

Then, from the sociomatrices, pupils sociometric scores were found. According to the pupils sociometric scores (total number of choices), pupils were classified into six categories. They were popular, above average, average, below average, neglectees, isolates, and rejectees. All pupils were classified in the following way.

Table 3.2: ***Classification according to sociometric scores***

Range	*Class*	
15 and above	Popular	(P)
11 to 14	Above average	(AA)
8 to 10	Average	(A)
4 to 7	Below average	(BA)
1 to 3	Neglectees	(N)
0	Isolates	(I)
3 and more X	Rejectees	(R)

For arriving at the socialization ability scores, the following formula suggested by 'Proctar and Lewis' (1951) was adopted.

$$\text{An Individual's choice status} = \frac{\text{Number of persons choosing the individual}}{N-1}$$

Where N is the number of persons in the group.

The individual's choice status indices were converted into percentage scores.

These percentage scores for the total sample of the junior college students, were arrived at and designated as 'socialization ability' scores.

While treating the data both the categorywise classification and socialization ability scores were used wherever necessary.

The sociometric test is designed to elicit the actual behaviour being studied, and in so far as it does this it is a valid measure of that behaviour. No reference to an outside criterion is made.

SCIENTIFIC ATTITUDE SCALE

The researcher selected Scientific Attitude Scale (SAS) constructed and standardised by J.K. Sood and R.J. Sanadhya.

The manual reports:

SAS consists of six dimensions, viz., rationality, open-mindedness, curiosity, aversion to superstitions, objectivity of intellectual beliefs, and suspended judgement.

Dimension 1: Rationality

a. Commitment of the value of rationality.
b. Tendency to test traditional beliefs.
c. Seeking for natural cause of events and identification of cause and effect relationship.
d. Acceptance of criticalness.
e. Challenge of authority.

Dimension 2: Curiosity

a. Desire for understanding new situations that are not explained by the existing body of knowledge.
b. Seeking to find out the 'why' and 'how' of observed phenomena.

c. Giving emphasis on the question in approach for novel situation.
d. Desire for completeness of knowledge.

Dimension 3: Open mindedness

a. Willingness to revise opinions and conclusions.
b. Desire for new things and ideas.
c. Rejection of singular and rigid approach to people, things and ideas.

Dimension 4: Aversion to superstitions

a. Rejection of superstitions and false beliefs.
b. Acceptance of scientific facts and explanation.

Dimension 5: Objectivity of intellectual beliefs

a. Demonstration of the greatest possible concern of observing and recording facts without any influence of personal pride, bias or ambition.
b. Not allowing any change in interpreting results on the basis of present social, economic or political influences.

Dimension 6: Suspended judgement

a. Unwillingness to draw inferences before evidence is collected.
b. Unwillingness to accept facts that are not supported by convincing proof.
c. Avoidance of quick judgement.

This Scientific Attitude Scale was constructed by following the Likert Method considering its advantages over other methods. This scale was prepared based on the contributions made by J.J. Schwab, J.S. Bruner, Bertrand Russell, William D. Romey, P.L. Gorder, Victor Y. Billech, Paul B. Diederich, Curtis, Noll, Haney E. Richard, etc.

Item Writing, Editing and Revision

An initial pool of 130 statements was prepared. This pool of statements was given to a panel of experienced and qualified teacher educators, after getting it's language pruned by experts. The experts were requested to rate each statement on three categories by answering the under mentioned questions.

Is the attitude/view measured by this item

- essential ?
- useful but not essential ? or
- not essential ?

After collecting the experts opinions on every statement, content validity ratios (C.V.R.) were calculated. Statements whose CVRs were more than or equal to 0.62 was significant at 0.05 level of significance for N = 10. In this way, the content validity of statements was ascertained quantitatively by utilizing Laushe's (1975) suggestion. Thus out of 130 statements, only 66 were retained for initial tryout.

Initial Tryout

Sixty-six statements of different dimensions of scientific attitude were arranged in Likert Method. Fifty per cent items were of positive polarity and remaining fifty per cent were of negative polarity. This instrument was administered on the sample and was asked to assign any one of the five categories after reading each statement carefully from SA to SD (Strongly agree to Strongly disagree) which are later scored using Likert technique with weighted scores 5 to 1.

For items of negative polarity, the scoring system was reversed. The 't' values for 66 statements were calculated to construct a final Scientific Attitude Scale.

The final form of the Scientific Attitude Scale (Appendix A) contained 36 statements, of which 18 are of positive polarity and 18 are of negative polarity. The distribution of items is given in Table 3.3.

The maximum and the minimum score of Scientific Attitude Scale is 180 and 36 respectively.

Table 3.3: ***Dimension-wise distribution of items— Scientific Attitude Scale***

Dimension	*Negative Polarity (Item Numbers)*	*Positive Polarity (Item Numbers)*
1. Rationality	1, 2, 6	3, 4, 5
2. Curiosity	8, 9	7, 10, 11, 12
3. Open-mindedness	13, 14	15, 16, 17, 18
4. Aversion to superstition	19, 21, 24	20, 22, 23
5. Objectivity of Intellectual beliefs	25, 26, 28, 30	27, 29
6. Suspended judgement	31, 32, 34, 35	33, 36

Internal Consistencies and Discriminative Validity

The reliability of Scientific Attitude Scale scores as calculated by split-half method is found to be 0.88. Scientific Attitude Scale was administered on a sample of 200 and this analysis provided information about the internal consistency and discriminant validity of the six dimensions of the scale. The results are summarized in Table 3.4.

SCIENCE ATTITUDE SCALE

To measure attitude towards science the investigator has used the science attitude scale prepared by Avinash Grewal (1977). The manual reports:

Technique Used

Likert method and scale discrimination techniques were considered to be more appropriate for use in the construction of Science Attitude Scale. The construction of the scale was done through several procedural steps.

Item Writing, Editing and Selection

Before preparing the Science Attitude Scale, the authors of the tool reviewed the relevant literature and other descriptive

Table 3.4: ***Reliability Coefficients for Six Dimensions of Scientific Attitude Scale***

Dimension	*No. of items*	*Reliability*	*Internal*		*Correlation*		*Co-efficient*	
			I	*II*	*III*	*IV*	*V*	*VI*
1. Rationality	6	0.76	1.0	0.35	0.31	0.34	0.33	0.32
2. Curiosity	6	0.86	3.5	1.0	5.3	4.8	0.5	0.53
3. Openmindedness	6	0.84	3.1	0.53	1.0	0.53	0.49	0.53
4. Aversion to Superstitions	6	0.80	0.34	0.48	0.53	1.00	0.57	0.53
5. Objectivity of intellectual beliefs	6	0.73	0.33	0.5	0.49	0.57	1.0	0.53
6. Suspended Judgement	6	0.82	0.32	0.5	0.53	0.53	0.63	1.0
7. Scientific (Total) Attitude Scale	36	0.86	0.62	0.76	0.8	0.81	0.85	0.82

material dealing with the contribution of scientific thought. Students studying science and arts subjects were also asked to give reasons for and against the study of science. Some of the statements used were obtained from the relevant scales prepared by Sood (1975) and Test on Understanding of Science (TOUS).

While preparing the items for this Scale, the criteria mentioned by Edward (1975) have been followed. Precautions were taken to keep the reading level of the scale well within the reach of the normative pupils. The universe of content for the attitude scale constituted forty-one statements about science, collected from various relevant sources dealing with the world of science. In the process of collecting, editing, and selecting the statement, the informal criteria as suggested by Wang (1932), Thurstone and Chave (1929), Likert (1932), Berd (1940), Edwards (1941), Zilling (1928), and Seeleman (1940) were carefully observed.

With a view to know the nature of the statements, the edited items were submitted to a group of five judges. These judges were specifically instructed to classify these forty-one statements into two piles on the strength of the nature of the statement, positive and negative. Classifying any one of these items into neutral category was discouraged. They were then requested to read the statements with a view to point out, if any, flaws, omissions, and commissions in the grammatical structure of the statements. Out of the forty-one items, eighteen were classified as positive while twenty-three as negative items. Suggestions offered by judges were incorporated in the statements and they were further refined and improved. For further elimination of some more items of the scale, discrimination technique developed by Edwards and Kilpatrick (1948) was used. The scale discrimination technique eliminates the least discriminating items which other methods, including Likert's judging technique, fails to do, omissions and commissions in the grammatical structure of the statements.

Having known the nature, these items were edited into five point scale after Likert, and were then administered to a class of hundred representative pupils with the standard instruction. Weightages were assigned, and values as well as chi-square values were calculated for item analysis purposes.

The chi-square values of the positive items were estimated to be 4.183 and 0.591 whereas of the negative items, they were found to be 3.667 and 0.445 respectively. Out of forty-one statements (18 positive, 23 negative), twenty items evenly distributed into four categories specified above, were retained for the final try out. While selecting the ten items from each category of statements, it was observed to select items with low Q-values and with scale value which were spread over the entire scale at relatively equally spaced distances along the psychological continuum.

Tryout and Final Form

Finally, the Science Attitude Scale (Appendix B) consisted of twenty items after dropping the lest discriminating items. The scale was then administered on 515 higher secondary students drawn from 6 schools of Bhopal. This was done with a view to determine the reliability, validity and norms of the scale.

Reliability

The reliability of the Attitude towards Science Scale was estimated by the authors by the split-half (0.86) and test-retest (0.75) methods which was reported to be quite satisfactory. The coefficient of correlation between Likert-Thurstone technique of scoring was also used. The reliability coefficients are given in Table 3.5.

Table 3.5: ***Reliability coefficients and the SEs of their measurements***

Method	*Reliability Coefficient*		*Reliability*	*SEs*
	Obtained	*Corrected*		*Measurement*
1. Split-Half (Oddeven)	0.76	0.86	0.87	–2.63
2. Test-retest (3 months)	0.60	0.75	0.77	–3.55
3. Likert-Thurstone (Technique of Scoring)	0.94	0.96	0.96	*4.48

Validity

The Science Attitude Scale reflects content validity and the method of selecting items supports this supposition. In addition, differences in mean scores were found by the authors of the tool among the selected groups of known preference for science, i.e., Arts (mean = 46.41) and Science (Mean = 50.58) students which is highly significant (t = 6.62) at 1 per cent level.

INTERPRETATION OF SCORES

Socialization Ability

1. On the basis of the total number of choices, the classification was made, as stated earlier.
2. To arrive at a 'socialization ability' score the formula already reported was adopted.

The socialization scores were used to calculate sub-sample means and standard deviations. The category wise classification was used to count the frequency of the individuals in each category and identify the nature of the distribution.

Scientific Attitude

The scientific attitude scores were interpreted as per Table 3.6.

Table 3.6: ***The Score Range and Interpretation of Scientific Attitude Score***

Score range	*Interpretation*	
36 - 53	Highly Negative	(HN)
54 - 89	Negative	(Neg)
90 - 125	Neutral	(N)
126 - 161	Positive	(P)
162 - 180	Highly Positive	(HP)

Science Attitude

The scores of attitude towards science were interpreted as per Table 3.7.

Table 3.7: ***The Score Range and Interpretation of Attitude Towards Science Score***

Score range	*Interpretation*	
0 - 10	Highly Negative	(HN)
11 - 30	Negative	(Neg)
31 - 50	Neutral	(N)
51 - 70	Positive	(P)
71 - 80	Highly Positive	(HP)

To enable the investigator to answer the research questions regarding the distribution of the three traits in the sample and to find whether there is association between the traits, the following declarative hypotheses were chosen.

SELECTION OF SAMPLE

As socialization ability can be measured in the context of a group only, the investigator had to resort to the technique of random selection of groups of 15 junior college students.

The area which is chosen for this investigation of sociometric analysis, is an urban area. Education wise, there are a number of junior colleges offering education at this level, in both residential and non residential systems. They provide instruction in Mother tongue and English also. The student population is mostly non local with students coming to study the intermediate course from various towns and villages. In all, the city has twenty-nine junior college; Fifteen groups of intermediate students were randomly selected from the above twenty-nine junior colleges. The groups were of varied sizes depending on the number of students in that class. Table 3.8 shows the group particulars and size.

ADMINISTRATION OF TOOLS

The three questionnaires, namely, sociometric questionnaires, attitude towards science scale, and scientific attitude scale were administered to 15 groups comprising of 446 pupils.

Before administering the questionnaire, the pupils were informed that their responses would be used only for purposes of

Table 3.8: *Student Sample*

S. No.	*Sex*	*Educational Discipline*	*R/N*	*E/T*	*N*
1.	Girls	Science	R	E	31
2.	Girls	Science	R	E	22
3.	Girls	Science	R	T	46
4.	Boys	Science	NR	E	56
5.	Girls	Arts	NR	T	37
6.	Boys	Science	R	E	46
7.	Boys	Science	R	T	24
8.	Coeducation	Science	NR	E	30
9.	Coeducation	Science	R	T	32
10.	Coeducation	Science	R	E&T	29 (17 + 12)
11.	Girls	Arts	NR	T	19
12.	Girls	Arts	NR	E	16
13.	Coeducation	Science	NR	E&T	26 (8 + 18)
14.	Coeducation	Arts	NR	T	16
15.	Coeducation	Science	NR	T	16

research and would be treated as strictly confidential. They were asked to be frank in their responses. They were also instructed to respond to all the items based on their expectations.

Sociometric questionnaire was administered along with scientific attitude and science attitude scales. The instructions were read out for all the three questionnaires. The pupils were directed to give their responses according to the instructions given.

As sociometric questionnaire is a friendships choice technique, care was also taken that most of the students were present in the class when the questionnaire was administered.

Scoring was done as per the instructions given in the manual.

STATISTICAL PROCEDURES

1. The level of significance chosen for interpreting the values is 0.01 level.
2. Score distributions are classified into categories. For attitudes, classification like highly negative, negative, neutral,

positive, and highly positive were used. For socialization ability, categories like popular, isolates, etc., were used.

3. Chi-square test of significance is used to verify normality of distribution and test of independence of traits.
4. For identifying the influencing variables, t-test was applied for comparing the mean differences in the sub-samples

4

Analysis of Data

The present investigation is a descriptive survey to study the socialization ability, scientific attitude, and attitude towards science of junior college students. It was conducted on a random sample of fifteen groups comprising of a total number of 446 students.

This investigation was conducted on post adolescent students and the investigator started with the working assumption that the three criterion traits will not be distributed normally among this student population. It was argued that with the influence of the peer groups, education environment, and home environment, students will attain socialization ability. It was also reasoned that scientific attitude and attitude towards science, which are the outcomes of science education, environment, and social interaction, will be distributed normally. This population was expected to possess high scientific attitude and positive attitude towards science.

Because of the common agencies, contributing to the development of the three traits, and the social contexts of expression of these attitudes, it was argued that there will be an association between the three traits of this study, namely, socialization ability, scientific attitude, and attitude towards science.

A triangular two way relationship between the three traits was expected to be present in some form or other.

The following hypotheses were formulated and the data gathered was analysed accordingly:

HYPOTHESES

1. The traits socialization ability, scientific attitude and attitude towards science will be distributed normally in the sample of junior college students.
2. The traits socialization ability scientific attitude, and attitude towards science will be associated with each other in this sample.
3. In all, the sub samples of junior college students there will be association between the three traits; socialization ability, scientific attitude, and attitude towards science.
4. The variables selected for the study, namely: sex, class environment, medium of learning, type of institution, and discipline will be the influencing variables of the three traits socialization ability, scientific attitude, and attitude towards science.

HYPOTHESIS I

The traits socialization ability, scientific attitude, and attitude towards science will be distributed normally in this sample of junior college students.

I.1 Socialization Ability Will be Distributed Normally in Junior College Students

Table 4.1 shows the percentage wise distribution of the trait socialization ability in the whole sample. The observed data was tested for divergence from those expected on the hypothesis of a normal distribution.

From Table 4.1 it can be seen that, in this sample 39% are possessing high socialization ability, as against the expected 16%. In the middle category, i.e., average socialization ability category, there are 45% of this sample as against the expected 68%. The distribution of this trait socialization ability in this sample is not normal.

Table 4.1 : *Socialization Ability in Junior College Students Percentage Wise Distribution of Trait—Whale Sample Data*

N = 446

Categories	*I Low*	*N*	*BA*	*A*	*A A*	*P High*	*Chi-Square Value*
Percentage of Expected Frequency	2	14	34	34	14	2	411.45*
Percentage of Observed frequency	5	11	28	17	20	19	

Hypothesis : Normal Distribution Hypothesis
df = 5; P at 0.01 level is 15.086
* means chi-square value is significant at 0.01 level.
Finding: Hypothesis is rejected

I.2. Scientific Attitude Will be Distributed Normally in Junior College Students.

Table 4.2 shows the percentage wise distribution of scientific attitude in the whole sample. The observed data was tested for divergence from those expected on the hypothesis of a normal distribution.

Table 4.2 : *Scientific Attitude in Junior College Students percentage wise Distribution—Whole Sample Data*

N = 446

Categories	*HN Low*	*Neg*	*Neu*	*P*	*HP High*	*Chi-Square Value*
Percentage of Expected Frequency	3	24	46	24	3	762.2*
Percentage of Observed frequency	–	1	17	76	6	

Hypothesis : Normal Distribution Hypothesis
df = 4; p at 0.01 level is 13.277
* means chi-square value is significant at 0.01 level.
Finding: Hypothesis is rejected

From Table 4.2 it can be seen that, in this sample 82% are possessing positive scientific attitude as against the expected 27% and 17% possess neutral scientific attitude, and only 1% is identified as possessing negative attitude.

From the trend of the data it is evident that the distribution of scientific attitude is not normal in this sample.

I.3. The Trait Attitude Towards Science Will be Distributed Normally in Junior College Students

Table 4.3 shows the percentage wise distribution of the trait attitude towards science in the whole sample. The observed data was tested for divergence from those expected on the hypothesis of a normal distribution.

Table 4.3: ***Attitude Towards Science in Junior College Students Percentage wise Distribution—Whole Sample Data***

N = 446

Categories	*HN Low*	*Neg*	*Neu*	*P*	*HP High*	*Chi-Square Value*
Percentage of Expected Frequency	3	24	46	24	3	433.03*
Percentage of Observed frequency	-	1	45	53	1	

Hypothesis: Normal Distribution Hypothesis
df = 4; P at 0.01 level is 13.277
* means chi-square value is significant at 0.05 level.
Finding: Hypothesis is rejected

In this sample, 54% are possessing positive attitude towards science. There is only 1% of the sample holding negative attitude to science. From the data it is evident that attitude towards science is not distributed normally in post adolescent junior college students.

Socialization ability, scientific attitude, and attitude towards science are not distributed normally in this sample. Hence, the hypothesis of this study, that they will be distributed normally is not accepted.

HYPOTHESIS II

"The socialization ability, scientific attitude and attitude towards science will be associated with each other in the sample."

II.1. The traits socialization ability and scientific attitude will be associated with each other in this sample of junior college students.

Table 4.4 which is a contigency table shows the observed frequency of percentage-wise distribution of the whole sample, for the traits socialization ability and scientific attitude and was used to apply the chi-square test of independence.

The hypothesis of independence of traits was used.

Table 4.4: ***Association of Socialization Ability and Scientific Attitude in Junior College Students Whole Sample Data— Scientific Attitude***

SOCIALIZATION ABILITY	*HN*	*N*	*Neutral*	*Positive*	*HP*	*Total*
P	-	-	4.29	13.77	1.35	19.41
AA	-	0.45	2.93	15.12	1.13	19.63
A	-	-	3.16	14.0	0.23	17.39
BA	-	0.23	3.39	21.90	2.03	27.55
N	-	-	2.03	7.22	1.35	10.60
ZI	-	-	1.35	3.84	0.23	5.42
Total		0.68	17.15	75.85	6.32	100.00

Figures in table are observed percentage frequencies

Hypothesis: Independence of traits

Chi-square value is 61.7*; df = 20; p at : 0.01 level is 37.566; obtained chi-square value is significant

Finding: Hypothesis rejected, there is association between socialization ability and scientific attitude

Hypothesis is rejected as obtained chisquare value is greater than the value at 0.01 level, i.e., 37.586. Hence there is an association between socialization ability and scientific attitude among Junior college students.

There are reasons to believe that socialization ability and scientific attitude are associated with each other. 82% of this sample possess positive scientific attitude, and 39% of this show high socialization ability. A very insignificant percentage of the sample shows low socialization ability and negative scientific attitude. From an examination of Table 4.4, it is seen that the trait association is evident in areas of high socialization ability and positive scientific attitude.

II.2. Socialization ability and attitude towards science will be associated with each other in junior college students.

Table 4.5 shows the percentage-wise distribution of association of the traits socialization ability and attitude towards science in the whole sample of this study.

The Hypothesis of independence of traits was adopted.

Table 4.5: ***Association of Socialization Ability and Attitude Towards Science in Junior College Students— Whole Sample Data***

Attitude Towards Science

SOCIALIZATION ABILITY	*HN*	*N*	*Neutral*	*Positive*	*HP*	*Total*
P	-	-	9	10.4	-	19.4
AA	-	0.2	9.2	10.1	-	19.5
A	-	-	7.7	9.7	-	17.4
BA	-	0.2	12.0	15.0	0.5	27.7
N	-	-	4.5	5.9	0.2	10.6
I	-	-	2.7	2.5	0.2	5.4
Total		0.4	45.1	53.6	0.9	100.00

Figures in table are observed percentage frequencies
Hypothesis: Independence of traits distribution
Chi-square value is 9.6; df = 20; P at : 0.01 level is 37.566;
obtained chi-square value is significant
Finding: Hypothesis accepted, there is no association between socialization ability and attitude towards science

Hence it is concluded that in this sample, the socialization ability and attitude towards science are not associated with each other.

II.3. The traits scientific attitude and attitude towards science will be associated with each other in junior college students.

Table 4.6 shows the percentage wise distribution of association of the traits scientific attitude and attitude towards science in the whole sample.

The Hypothesis of independence of traits was followed in Table 4.6.

Table 4.6: ***Association of Scientific Attitude and Attitude Towards Science in Junior College Students Whole Sample Data***

Scientific Attitude

ATTITUDE TOWARDS SCIENCE	*HN*	*N*	*Neutral*	*Positive*	*HP*	*Total*
HN	-	-	-	-	-	-
N	-	0.45	-	-	-	0.45
Neutral	-	0.23	9.93	34.32	0.68	45.16
Positive	-	-	7.22	41.08	5.19	53.49
HP	-	-	-	0.48	0.48	0.90
Total		0.68	17.15	75.85	6.32	100.00

Figures in table are observed percentage frequencies

Hypothesis: Independence of traits distribution

Chi-square value is 35.4; df = 16; P at : 0.01 level is 32; obtained chi-square value is significant

Finding: Hypothesis rejected, there is no association between socialization ability and attitude towards science

From Table 4.6 it can be found that chi-square value is significant at 0.01 level. There are reasons to believe that in this sample, attitude towards science and scientific attitude are associated. From an examination of the contingency table, it can seen that 82% of this sample of post adolescents hold positive scientific attitude and 54% hold favourable attitude towards science.

Hence, in the Junior college students who are in post adolescent stage :

a. There is association between socialization ability and scientific attitude.
b. There is no association between socialization ability and attitude towards science.
c. There is association between scientific attitude and attitude towards science.

HYPOTHESIS III

"In all the sub samples, there will be association between the three traits, socialization ability, scientific attitude and attitude towards science."

The sample of students were sub divided according to the variables. The variables of the study, the categories in each variable and sample size are given below.

Table 4.7: ***Variable Wise Sample Description***

S.No.	*Variable*	*Category*	*Number*
1.	Sex	Male	213
		Female	233
2.	Class Environment	Non-Residential	273
		Residential	173
3.	Medium of Learning	English	226
		Telugu	220
4.	Type of Institution	Co-education	149
		Uni-sex Institutions	297
5.	Discipline	Science	358
		Arts	88

From each of the sub samples, contingency tables were drawn. By applying the test of independence of traits, Chi-square values were calculated and consolidated tables of chi-square values were calculated and consolidated tables of chi-square values are presented. The percentage contingency tables, where trait associations are found, are given below.

Table 4.8: ***Percentage-wise Contingency Tables Showing the Association between Socialization Ability and Scientific Attitude in the Sub Sample—Science***

Scientific Attitude

SOCIALIZATION ABILITY	*HN*	*N*	*Neutral*	*Positive*	*HP*	*Total*
P	-	-	4.19	14.53	1.68	20.40
AA	-	0.56	2.23	15.92	1.12	19.83
A	-	-	2.23	12.29	0.28	14.80
BA	-	0.28	3.91	21.79	2.51	28.49
N	-	-	2.23	7.54	1.68	11.45
I	-	-	0.84	4.19	-	5.03
Total	-	0.84	15.63	76.26	7.27	100.00

Table 4.9: ***Percentage-wise Contingency Tables Showing the Association Between Socialization Ability and Scientific Attitude in the Sub Sample—Arts***

Scientific Attitude

SOCIALIZATION ABILITY	*HN*	*N*	*Neutral*	*Positive*	*HP*	*Total*
P	-	-	4.70	10.59	-	15.29
AA	-	-	5.88	11.76	1.18	18.22
A	-	-	7.06	21.18	-	28.24
BA	-	-	1.18	22.35	-	23.53
N	-	-	1.18	5.88	-	7.06
I	-	-	3.53	2.35	1.18	7.06
Total	-	-	23.53	74.11	2.36	100.00

Table 4.10: ***Percentage-wise Contingency Table Showing the Association between Scientific Attitude and Attitude Towards Science in the Sub Sample—Boys***

Attitude Towards Science	Scientific Attitude					
	HN	*N*	*Neutral*	*Positive*	*HP*	*Total*
HN	-	-	-	-	-	-
N	-	0.48	-	-	-	0.48
Neutral	-	-	7.73	29.09	1.36	38.18
Positive	-	-	7.27	47.27	5.90	60.44
HP	-	-	-	0.45	0.45	0.90
Total	-	0.48	15.00	76.81	7.71	100.00

Table 4.11: ***Percentage-wise Contingency Tables Showing the Association between Scientific Attitude and Attitude Towards Science in the Sub Sample—Girls***

Attitude Towards Science	Scientific Attitude					
	HN	*N*	*Neutral*	*Positive*	*HP*	*Total*
HN	-	-	-	-	-	-
N	-	0.45	-	-	-	0.45
Neutral	-	0.45	12.11	39.46	-	52.02
Positive	-	-	7.17	34.98	4.48	46.63
HP	-	-	-	0.45	0.45	0.90
Total	-	0.90	19.28	74.89	4.93	100.00

Table 4.12: ***Percentage-wise Contingency Tables Showing the Association between Scientific Attitude and Attitude Towards Science in the Sub Sample—Non-Residential***

Scientific Attitude

ATTITUDE TOWARDS SCIENCE	*HN*	*N*	*Neutral*	*Positive*	*HP*	*Total*
HN	-	-	-	-	-	-
N	-	0.82	-	-	-	0.82
Neutral	-	-	10.21	36.33	-	46.54
Positive	-	-	5.71	40.41	5.71	51.82
HP	-	-	-	0.41	0.41	0.82
Total	-	0.82	15.92	77.15	6.11	100.00

Table 4.13: ***Percentage-wise Contingency Tables Showing the Association between Scientific Attitude and Attitude Towards Science in the Sub Sample—Telugu Medium***

Scientific Attitude

ATTITUDE TOWARDS SCIENCE	*HN*	*N*	*Neutral*	*Positive*	*HP*	*Total*
HN	-	-	-	-	-	-
N	-	0.88	-	-	-	0.88
Neutral	-	-	10.57	36.56	-	47.13
Positive	-	-	9.69	37.01	4.41	51.11
HP	-	-	-	0.44	0.44	0.88
Total	-	0.88	20.26	74.01	4.85	100.00

Table 4.14: ***Percentage-wise Contingency Tables Showing the Association between Scientific Attitude and Attitude Towards Science in the Sub Sample—Co-Education***

Scientific Attitude

ATTITUDE TOWARDS SCIENCE	*HN*	*N*	*Neutral*	*Positive*	*HP*	*Total*
HN	-	-	-	-	-	-
N	-	1.35	-	-	-	1.35
Neutral	-	-	5.40	30.40	0.68	36.48
Positive	-	-	7.43	48.65	4.73	60.81
HP	-	-	-	0.68	0.68	1.36
Total	-	1.35	12.83	79.73	6.09	100.00

Table 4.15: ***Percentage-wise Contingency Tables Showing the Association between Scientific Attitude and Attitude Towards Science in the Sub Sample—Science***

Scientific Attitude

ATTITUDE TOWARDS SCIENCE	*HN*	*N*	*Neutral*	*Positive*	*HP*	*Total*
HN	-	-	-	-	-	-
N	-	0.56	-	-	-	0.56
Neutral	-	0.28	8.65	30.45	0.56	39.94
Positive	-	-	6.98	45.25	6.15	58.38
HP	-	-	-	0.56	0.56	1.12
Total	-	0.84	15.63	76.26	7.27	100.00

III.1. In all the sub samples of junior college students there will be association between socialization ability and scientific attitude.

Table 4.16 shows chi-square values for the association between the traits socialization ability and scientific attitude in the variables wise sub samples.

Table 4.16: *Association between Traits Socialization Ability and Scientific Attitude in Sub-Samples of Junior College Students*

	Variable	*Sub-Sample*	*Chi-Square Values*
1.	Sex	Boys	4.74
		Girls	20.56
2.	Class Environment	Residential	19.25
		Non-Residential	28.32
3.	Medium of Learning	English	18.3
		Telugu	25.31
4.	Type of Institution	Co-education	15.61
		Uni-sex Institutions	20.76
5.	Discipline	Science	54.97 *
		Arts	74.86 *

*Denotes the chi-square value is significant at 0.01 level

Hypothes s : Independence of traits distribution
df = 16; P at 0.01 level is 32

Finding : a. Two values are significant at 0.01 level
b. Socialization ability and scientific attitude are associated in subsamples of Science students and Arts Students

As seen trom Table 4.16, in only two subsamples the traits socialization ability and scientific attitude are associated with each other. The subsamples are related to the variable 'discipline'. So, the Hypothesis is accepted in some subsamples. The traits socialization ability and scientific attitude are not associated in the subsamples sex, type of institution, medium of learning, and class environment.

The traits socialization ability and scientific attitude are showing association in the subsamples of Science and Arts.

III.2. In all the subsamples of junior college students there will be association between socialization ability and attitude towards science.

Table 4.17: ***Association between Traits Socialization Ability and Attitude Towards Science in Subsamples of Junior College Students***

	Variable	*Sub-Sample*	*Chi-Square Values*
1.	Sex	Boys	11.17
		Girls	19.84
2.	Class Environment	Residential	18.05
		Non-Residential	14.19
3.	Medium of Learning	English	13.35
		Telugu	12.85
4.	Type of Institution	Co-education	9.21
		Uni-sex Institutions	15.76
5.	Discipline	Science	12.55
		Arts	10.25

Hypothesis : Independence of traits distribution

df = 20; P at 0.01 level is 37.566

Finding: a. All the values are not significant at 0.01 level

b. Socialization ability and attitude towards science are not associated in all the sub samples.

As seen from Table 4.17 in all the sub samples, the traits socialization ability and attitude towards science are not associated with each other. So the Hypothesis is rejected.

III.3. In all the sub samples of Junior College Students there will be association between scientific attitude and Attitude towards science.

Table 4.18: ***Association Between traits Scientific Attitude and Attitude Towards Science in Sub Samples of Junior College Students***

Variable	*Sub-Sample*	*Chi-Square Values*
1. Sex	Boys	210.06 *
	Girls	131.95 *
2. Class Environment	Residential	10.25
	Non-Residential	223.43 *
3. Medium of Learning	English	16.98
	Telugu	40.51 *
4. Type of Institution	Co-education	157.35
	Uni-sex Institutions	21.89
5. Discipline	Science	225.93 *
	Arts	0.34

*Denotes that chi-square value is significant at 0.01 level.

Hypothesis : Independence of traits distribution

df = 20; p at 0.01 level is 37.586

Finding : a. Six values are significant at 0.01 level.

b. Scientific attitude and attitude towards science are associated in sub samples of Boys, Girls, Co-education, Telugu Medium, Non-residential institution, and Science students.

As seen from Table 4.18 the traits scientific attitude and Attitude towards science are associated with each other in 'six' sub samples. The traits scientific attitude and attitude towards science show association in the subsamples : 'Boys', 'Girls', 'Co-education', 'Telugu Medium Students', 'Non-Residential' and 'Science Students'.

The traits scientific attitude and attitude towards science are not associated in the sub samples of Uni-sex institution', 'English medium', 'Residential', and 'Arts students.

Hence, in the junior college students, who are in post adolescent stage.

a. There is association between socialization ability and scientific attitude in some sub samples.
b. There is no association between socialization ability and attitude towards science in all the sub samples of the study.
c. There is association between scientific attitude and attitude towards science in some sub samples.

Hypothesis IV

"The variables selected for the study will be the influencing variables of the three traits—socialization ability, scientific attitude and attitude towards science."

The subsample means and standard deviations are calculated and the significance of the difference between means was computed by applying the t-test.

IV.1. The variables, sex, type of institution, medium of learning, class environment, and discipline are influencing the trait socialization ability.

Table 4.19 shows the sub sample means and standard deviations for each variable and the 't' value for the trait 'socialization ability'.

Table 4.19: ***Socialization Ability—Variable Analysis Data***

Variable	*Sub-Sample*	*N*	*Mean*	*S.D.*	SE_D	*t*
Sex	Male	213	17.02	13.43	1.51	4.64*
	Female	233	24.02	18.26		
Class Environ-	Non-Residential	273	22.88	16.38	1.4	3.28*
	Residential	173	18.29	16.36		

Table 4.19: *(Contd.)*

Variable	*Sub-Sample*	*N*	*Mean*	*S.D.*	SE_D	*t*
Medium of Learning	English	226	19.23	16.59	1.58	2.15
	Telugu	220	22.66	16.69		
Type of Institution	Co-education	149	25.3	16.3	1.65	2.15
	Uni-sex Institutions	297	18.99	16.55		
Discipline	Science	358	18.87	14.81	2.24	2.89*
	Arts	88	27.58	19.64		

*Denotes that 't' value is significant at 0.01 level

Findings : Four t' values are significant

As seen from Table 4.19, four 't' values are significant at 0.01 level. Hence it is concluded that the variables sex, class environment, type of institution, and discipline are influencing the trait socialization ability.

The findings are :

1. The girl students of this sample of junior college students show better socialization ability than boy students.
2. Students of non-residential colleges show better socialization ability than students of residential colleges.
3. Students of co-educational colleges show better socialization ability than students of uni-sex institutions.
4. Students of 'Arts' discipline show better socialization ability than Science students.

IV. 2. The variables, sex, medium of learning, class environment, and discipline are influencing the trait scientific attitude.

Table 4.20 shows the sub-sample means and standard deviations for each variable and the 't' values for the trait 'scientific attitude'.

Table 4.20: *Scientific Attitude-Variable Analysis Data*

Variable	*Sub-Sample*	*N*	*Mean*	*S.D.*	SE_D	*t*
Sex	Male	213	139.53	15.20		
					1.51	1.52
	Female	233	137.23	16.77		
Class Environ-ment	Non-Residential	273	139.3	16.39	1.78	1.71
	Residential	173	136.26	19.37		
Medium of Learning	English	226	140.43	17.44	1.58	2.41
	Telugu	220	136.62	15.80		
Type of Institution	Co-education	149	140.32	14.95	1.52	1.88
	Uni-sex Institutions	297	137.45	15.53		
Discipline	Science	358	139.40	15.75		
					1.76	2.03
	Arts	88	135.82	14.52		

Findings : all the values are not significant.

As seen from Table 4.20 none of the 't' values are significant at '0.01' level. Hence it is concluded that the variables : Sex, Residence, Class environment, Medium of learning, Type of institution, College, and Discipline are not influencing the trait scientific attitude.

IV. 3. The variable, sex, type of institution, medium of learning, class environment, and discipline are influencing the trait attitude towards science.

Table 4.21 shows the sub sample means and standard deviations for each variable and the 't' value for the trait attitude towards science.

Table 4.21: ***Attitude Towards Science-Variable Analysis Data***

Variable	*Sub-Sample*	*N*	*Mean*	*S.D.*	SE_D	*t*
Sex	Male	213	51.43	6.73	0.68	1.5
	Female	233	50.41	7.65		
Class Environment	Non-Residential	273	50.54	7.20	0.7	1.68
	Residential	173	51.72	7.29		
Medium of Learning	English	226	51.39	6.94	0.81	0.39
	Telugu	220	51.07	9.9		
Type of Institution	Co-education	149	51.99	7.6	1.79	8.29*
	Uni-sex Institution	297	66.83	28.9		
Discipline	Science	358	64.0	22.76	1.37	12.39*
	Arts	88	47.03	6.21		

*Denotes that 't' value is significant at 0.01 level.

Findings : Two values are significant.

As seen from Table 4.21 two 't' values are significant at '0.01' level. Hence it is concluded that the variables 'type of Institution' and 'Discipline' are influencing the trait Attitude towards science.

The findings are :

1. Students of unisex institutions show better attitude towards science than students of coeducation colleges.
2. 'Science' students hold better attitude towards science than 'Arts' students.

The conclusions drawn on the basis of analysis and discussion are presented in the following chapter.

5

Findings and Discussion

This study of the socialization ability, scientific attitude, and attitude towards science among junior college students was taken up with the assumption that the three traits will be associated with each other.

It was hypothesized that the socialization ability and scientific attitude will be associated and also socialization ability and attitude towards science will be associated. It was further hypothesized that in this sample of junior college students, scientific attitude and attitude towards science will be associated.

The working assumption underlying the formulation of the above hypotheses regarding the association of traits was the common origin and development of these traits which is in turn rooted in the education environment, i.e., school and educational peer groups. This is a sample of post adolescent students undergoing education with ambitions about future. The general age group is 17+ and in another four to five years this kind of college population, will acquire all their socialization skills, will acquire the necessary educational qualification to earn bread and butter and will be a participant in the society. The modern society needs persons who are highly talented, and who have enough of sociability to maintain the social structure.

To prepare the individual for proper social functioning and social contribution, the education process as already pointed out plays a very vital role. In fact, over and above the cognitive and psychomotor skills, the role of education in contributing to the effective growth of the individual by developing a value system and developing the right attitudes cannot be questioned. The modern society requires individuals with favourable attitude towards science because the modern society is primarily progressive and technological.

It was hypothesized that, because the sample of this study has passed through the various stages of schooling, and exposed to the benefits of science and technology, it will automatically develop a favourable attitude towards science. The origin of these attitudes is in school, and environment. But the Indian society, which is a changing one may consist of a population, which is not totally favourable to science. It may also be true with regard to this sample of students.

The major outcome of the educational process, especially learning of science is the development of scientific attitude. An individual with a scientific attitude is acknowledged as a useful member of the society, because of the personal characteristics he possesses, namely, rationality of thought, curiosity, open mindedness, aversion to superstition, objectivity of intellectual beliefs, and suspended judgement.

An individual with a combination of the above qualities is a useful leader, peer group member, and a follower. These are all qualities useful in a democratic social environment.

The main assumption of this study was that, in this sample of post adolescent junior college students, all the three traits will be associated with each other.

FINDINGS

The percentage of rejectees in the whole sample is 19.64. For further analysis, only those students with positive socialization ability were considered.

The analysis of data led the investigator to draw the following conclusions.

I. All the Three Traits are not Distributed Normally

a. The Trait Socialization Ability is not Distributed Normally

The socialization ability scores, which are expected to be

distributed normally along the scale 'Isolate' to 'Populars', are differing significantly from the expected situation. The trend of Socialization ability scores is skewed towards the 'Above Average to Popular' categories. This suggests, this sample of junior college students acknowledge the importance of the process of socialization by identifying certain fellow students as being above average or popular.

This trend is probably because the Junior college students do not like to work in isolation, rather they work in groups, move in groups, sit together, and even dine together.

In the adolescent age groups, students like to share their problems and issues and prefer to work together. Peer group effect is more evident at this age level. Adolescents are being influenced much by their peer group and they take the attitudes of the peer group as their own. Because of these reasons, this sample of junior college students have their preferences to most of their class mates, as their seating, working and eating companions, resulting in more of above average and populars in this sample. Hence a significant percentage of the sample shows high socialization ability.

b. The Trait Scientific Attitude is not Distributed Normally

The scientific attitude scores which are expected to be distributed normally along the scale highly negative to highly positive are differing significantly from the expected situation. The trend of occurrence of scientific attitude scores is towards positive scientific attitude, than normally expected. This suggests, this sample of junior college students have acquired better scientific attitude.

A very high percentage of these junior college students exhibited positive scientific attitudes. The scientific attitude is composed of rationality, curiosity, open mindedness, aversion to superstitions, objectivity of intellectual beliefs, and suspended judgement. Interestingly, these post adolescent students have very high level of curiosity. Their range of curiosity extends from day to day events to discoveries and advancements in science. It is evident from their reaction that a person should strive to know the secrets after observing some astonishing situations like magic. At the same time, their keenness of curiosity can be understood from their ideas that, scientists should make all efforts in collecting complete information about Mars. A strong curiosity to know biological events is also seen, which is deduced from their confidence in science and it's ability to forecast the sex of a foetus, while they know that scientists should be curious. Apparently they seem to be as curious as scientists, because of their feeling that students should be eager to conduct new experiments.

Another significant characteristic of these students is their suspended judgement, which is one of the most important aspects of scientific attitude. An individual with this quality avoids quick judgement, draws inferences only after evidence is collected, and accepts those facts alone that are supported by convincing proofs.

It is interesting to note that these students opine that more importance should be given to new discoveries of science than the traditional beliefs. This is very significant in he context of Indian Society where traditional beliefs are prevalent and influencing. Interestingly, these students know and are convinced that due to fast explosion of knowledge, facts and theories which stand true today may be disproved tomorrow. Their attitude towards traditional beliefs and scientific discoveries is commendable. When traditional beliefs and scientific discoveries are conflicting, they prefer accepting scientific discoveries. Their belief that all are equal before science deserves to be acknowledged and their feeling that failure is as important as success in scientific discoveries is noteworthy. These were evident from their feelings, that a science teacher should discuss the possible causes of a failed demonstration, and seniority and age of a scientist need not come in the way of a junior from raising doubts.

The sample of post adolescent students are more open minded and are objective in their beliefs. They believe that positive criticism benefits the advancement of knowledge and student should be willing to change the ideas if sufficient evidences about the hollowness of his ideas are available. They feel that modification of erroneous concepts should be done if some body presents the correct and fully tested facts and, in the light of new knowledge, one should be ready to change his prevalent misconceptions. These beliefs of the intermediate students which are indicative of their open mindedness have long reaching education implications. The modern Indian society needs citizens who are open minded and who are not hasty in jumping to conclusions. Fortunately, the student population appears to possess these qualities. This category of students are educable because of their open mindedness and ability to suspend judgement.

Objectivity of intellectual beliefs is another preferable dimension of scientific attitude. Such an individual will not allow extraneous influences on interpreting results. Because of the influence of present social, economic or political aspects he is not willing to change and interpret the results. He is equally objective and demonstrates the greatest possible concern for observing and recording facts. He is objective to the extent of not allowing the influence of personal pride, bias or ambition on the above. These students do seem to have objectivity of intellectual beliefs because, they know that evidence supporting a certain idea, should be provided, before the idea is accepted and that the scientists should draw inferences only on the basis of accurate observation. They have also demonstrated this quality when they said that people should not read only those news papers which are in consonance with their political ideologies and bribing should not stop a scientist from disclosing the research findings about the adverse effects of some discovery.

Rationality which is a commitment of an individual to a value means a tendency to test traditional beliefs, readiness to challenge authority, and acceptance of criticalness. Rationality involves seeking for natural cause of events and identification of cause and effect relationship. The junior college students in post adolescent stage are rational, as they believe that an idea should not be accepted if it is proved to be poor and a conclusion based on insufficient evidence should neither be accepted nor be rejected. They want the scientists to find out the occurrences of the undesired events in nature.

Peculiarly, these students are not completely averse to superstitions. They do react to a professed statement of a superstition by saying that it is a superstitious act but they do believe that it is impossible to defy widely held assumptions in society since very long time. They partially demonstrate their superstitions in their silent acceptance of astrology, and divine attribute to diseases.

It is possible that over and above the effect of the peer group on the development of attitude towards science the deep rooted parental authority is contributing to this inability to free themselves from superstitions.

The Indian home and the parents are well known for their deep rooted, inherent traditions which are full of superstitions carried from generation to generation and maintained within their community. But for this, the rest of the scientific attitude development in these post adolescent college students appears to be good.

c. Attitude Towards Science is not Distributed Normally

Attitude towards science scores which are expected to be distributed normally along the scale from highly negative to highly positive are differing significantly from the expected situation. The trend of occurrence of attitude towards science scores is towards moderate attitude than normally expected. This suggests that this sample of junior college students have moderate attitude towards science. When such large number of the junior college students show a positive level of scientific attitude, it is but natural to expect them to show a favourable attitude towards science. But only half of them admit that they hold favourable attitude to science. Peculiarly they did not have very strong attitude in this direction on any of the statements. They are aware that science sharpens one's reasoning power and logical thinking. It is noteworthy to observe that, for them, study of science subjects is not a dull affair and science provides more relationship than other subjects. Another significant attitude is that to them science is useful, for getting a success in the competitive examination. They are aware that science has turned the impossibilities into possibilities.

But, their other attitude responses towards science are more significant than the ones already pointed out. They think that science has made us to depend entirely on machines and admit that scientific knowledge alone cannot improve a man's life. They are afraid that science is bound to lead our society into godlessness. To them science subjects are very difficult to study. They think that science fails to solve all our problems. They believe that science alone is responsible for our progress. They are not sure whether scientific careers are more useful than other careers and almost admit that knowledge of science is not necessary for other subjects.

Another reason may be that the past academic environment, i.e., at primary and secondary levels is not helpful in developing a favourable attitude towards science. All the school subjects especially science and mathematics contribute to the development of favourable attitude towards school subjects. Attitude towards science is an academic attitude. Similarly all school subjects contribute to scientific attitude. Of course science and mathematics play vital role, but language studies help in developing creativity, environmental studies, i.e., studying social environment helps in widening the horizons of knowledge thus enabling the individual to be democratic, open minded, rational, secular, objective, accommodative, adjustable, and free from superstitions. While the school subjects seem to be developing these attitudes, which are a part and parcel of scientific attitude, it is surprising to note that the students are not favourably disposed to science subjects as a whole. Their feeling that science is difficult is a point worth analysing. It could be that the science class rooms are authoritarian. It could be that science teacher is not taking enough precaution to make the subject interesting or even developing a fear complex among the students by giving an impression that science is difficult.

Science is not a difficult subject. Science is a way of thought. It is a method of acquiring knowledge. Science is nothing but understanding nature. It involves learning by doing. Probably the science teachers are doing none of these things by not striving to impress upon their students about the nature of science. The student should learn about the importance of science and the nature of science. Then only he can develop a more favourable attitude towards science. It is suggested that a study of the Indian class rooms and teachers regarding the techniques and strategies they are using for developing favourable attitude towards various disciplines may throw useful light.

As a matter of fact in this sample, the percentage of individuals holding negative scientific attitude and unfavourable attitude towards science is significantly low. Though not distributed normally, the attitude towards science in this sample of junior college students is only moderate.

II. In this sample, there is an association between the three traits, namely, socialization ability, scientific attitude and attitude towards science. But these are not directly associated with each other

a. As far as this sample of junior college students is concerned, there are evidences of association between socialization ability and scientific attitude.
b. There are no evidences of association between socialization ability and attitude towards science.
c. There are reasons to believe that, scientific attitude and attitude towards science are associated with each other in this sample.

The above trend of attitudes towards science appears to be the reason, for nearly half of these college students not holding favourable attitude towards science. This raises the interesting question of why the students have positive Scientific Attitudes and do not have favourable attitude to science? There is no doubt that attitude towards science and scientific attitude are associated. The influence of science education, media, and teacher on the development of scientific attitude is well recognized. The students who are highly sociable are the products of primary and secondary education in our schools.

Science pervades our society. It too, is essentially a human activity, the product of exchanges and interactions between the individuals in a class room, and the environment. Science is socially constructed like other forms of knowledge. The most useful contribution of science education is scientific attitude. Science is more useful to an individual for its method; constant use of scientific method and thought leads to an individual with scientific attitude.

It is to be deemed that the present day school and society are successfully contributing to socialization and scientific attitude. For these students their peer groups are the nucleus of their society from which they relate themselves to the various societal aspects. Hence it is to be understood that these peer groups are functional, effective, and contributory to the development of the students. The education implications can be that the school, teachers, and parents should know the dynamics of these peer groups. They should also be willing to identify the isolates and rejectees, find out the reasons and adopt remedial programmes.

Improvement in socialization ability may help the student to successively participate in the education process for survival in the competitive world. The junior college student is in this stage of competition. He plans for future vocations. But again one has to come back to the question of why these students do not hold favourable attitude to science. Probably the traditional constraints in the society, social backwardness, religious influences on the individual or even the peer group influences may be the causes. Hence this duality of attitudes regarding scientific attitude and attitude towards science.

Throughout the discussion it was evident that socialization ability, scientific attitude, and attitude towards science have common origins. All of them appear to be the outcomes of the process of social inter action which may be planned or unplanned. Peer group and socialization ability are interdependent scientific attitude is an outcome of social interaction in classrooms. Attitude towards science is an outcome of their exposure to science while acquiring socialization ability and scientific attitude. In spite of the discrepancy in attitude towards science and scientific attitude, all the three concepts of this study, seem to be sociologically interrelated. A more detailed investigation of sociological influences on these three aspects may throw more light on their origin and development.

Indian population has its learnings towards spiritualism and the present day Indian society is an amalgam of materialistic spiritualism and idealism. The population is still in the stage of developing and improving its attitude towards science. Hence the type and nature of attitude towards science held by Indian students cannot be similar to those hold by their western counterparts. It has to be remembered that these students mostly belong to traditional backgrounds, and even if they are professing modernity, they lag behind in practising modernity. Modernization is known to influence the attitudes, and attitude towards science cannot be an exception to the influence of modernization process.

III. There are reasons to believe that the independent variables selected for the study are having influence on the distribution of the traits in sub samples.

a. In all the sub samples of the variables the association of the traits socialization ability and attitude towards science is not evident.

b. Variation in the trait association in the sub samples was found with reference to trait association between socialization ability and scientific attitude.

The sub-samples in terms of medium of learning, sex, class environment, and type of institutions indicate independent distribution of the traits socialization ability and scientific attitude. When the classification was in terms of discipline, trait association was found.

c. Variation in trait association in the sub samples was found in trait association between scientific attitude and attitude towards science.

The following sub-samples showed association between scientific attitude and attitude towards science. They are: science students, students learning through Telugu medium, i.e., mother tongue, girls sample, boys sample, students in coeducational institutions, and sample of students from non residential colleges.

a. Of the five selected variables of the study, it is found that scientific attitude is not influenced by any of them.

Five common variables were chosen for studying their influence on the traits. It was assumed that science students will be possessing better scientific attitude than arts students. Surprisingly, this was not found to be an influencing variable. This speaks good of the previous education because selection of disciplines commences only at the Intermediate stage. Women were assumed to be more superstitious and conservative. So it was felt that sex will be an influencing variable on scientific attitude. But it is satisfying to observe that boys and girls do not differ in their level of scientific attitudes. Learning through mother tongue is supposed to enable an individual to learn and think of the implications of science better, thus leading to the possession of better scientific attitude than those learning science through English which is not their mother tongue. But this variable is not influencing the scientific attitude among the junior college students. Similarly, the variables coeducation and student's residential status are not influencing the scientific attitude of the post adolescent students.

b. *The variables, discipline, sex, co-education, student's residential status were found to be influencing socialization.*

The findings are:

i. Arts students show better socialization ability than science students.

Presumingly, the kind of education the person receives influences his socialization ability. Students who study arts subjects may be less rigid, less confirming and less authoritarian than those studying science subjects. As competition is more stiffer for science students than arts students it is obvious that they are more study oriented and career oriented. This may lead to the reduced social interaction, inter personal jealousies, and probably there will not be close proximity with science students. These might have been the reasons for the better Socialization Ability of arts students than science students.

ii. Girls show better Socialization Ability than boys.

Girls, tend to be voluble, share their secrets, generally converse in peer group and usually share their problems. Girls also have a tendency to confide in their friends whereas boys do not confide so easily. Even though boys mix in their peer group, they feel that they will be looked down if others come to know of their problems. So these boys try to avoid the group and become 'neglectees' or 'isolates' or even 'rejectees'. This may be the reason for the low socialization ability of boys than girls.

iii. Students of co-education institution show better socialization ability than students of unisex institutions.

In co-educational institutions boys and girls work together and this mixing of both the sexes makes them converse freely with each other. The atmosphere is free to do group work or for groups interaction, whereas in unisex institutions, there may be less of interaction. Because of these reasons, students of co-educational institutions may be showing better Socialization Ability.

iv. Students of non residential institutions show better socialization ability than residential students.

Non-residential students or boarders spend their life together even after the college and they stay together during night time also. This close proximity may some times lead to rivalries. As this is the gang age, pupils band themselves together in groups and the prejudices and tensions involved may lead to group rivalries or clashes. Added to this there will be unhealthy competitions as they spend more time together. But day scholars have time to converse only during intervals and between the class hours, and time of inter action is less, and most probably there will be healthy conversation. This might have been the reason for better socialization ability of students of non-residential colleges.

v. The variable medium of learning is not an influencing variable on socialization ability.

Students irrespective of their medium of learning generally converse in their mother tongue. Probably this might have been the reason for the above finding.

c. The trait attitude towards science is influenced by two variables, namely, discipline and class environment.

The findings are :

1. Science students hold a more favourable attitude towards

science than arts students.

The above finding is an obvious one.

ii. Students of uni-sex institutions are better than the students of co-educational institutions as far as attitude towards science is concerned.

DISCUSSION

Post adolescent stage is a critical stage in the life or an individual. There, the 'individual is on the verge of the adulthood, ready to face the challenges of life, take up vocational responsibilities, and fulfil life aspirations' This stage is more stressful to the post-adolescent student who is on the verge of planning for vocational education. For Indian students this stage in their education career occupies highest significance. Along with his ambitions he has to fulfil the parental ambitions, compete with the general student population, compete within the peer group, and come out successfully in life.

Psychologically speaking the socialization ability of an individual and qualities like applying scientific method, to personal and day to day problems can be helpful to the individual in successfully passing through this phase.

Educationists are of the opinion that socialization ability and the scientific attitude are useful assets to an individual. Parallely the favourable attitude towards technological changes which are the outcomes of science—otherwise called as favourable attitude towards science can also be an asset to the individual.

It was pointed out in the earlier chapters that there is a likelihood that these traits, i.e., socialization ability scientific attitude and attitude towards science may be associated with each other because of their common origin, namely, school, peer group, home, and society.

The present study which was taken up to verify this hypothesis of the association between these three traits has resulted in the answer that there is association. The socialization ability and scientific attitude show association in this population of post adolescent students. The trait scientific attitude and attitude towards science also show association. But, there were no evidences of association between socialization ability and attitude towards science.

The hypothesis of triangular association between the traits is not established. This leads to the discussion of the common origin of these traits of the study. There is no doubt that the socialization ability of an individual mainly develops in the school and peer group. The scientific attitude is developed both in the school and the home. The attitude towards science is developed as an outcome of liking towards science subject, vocational ambitions in the field of science, and maybe to a certain extent peer group influence. Thus the development of scientific attitude as contributed by the school is mainly through learning of science and home influence where convention and traditions are followed and religious beliefs are learnt and practiced.

In the Indian context there is always a clash between science and religion. The population is generally believed to have low scientific attitude. It is not out of the way to point out that the scientific attitude studies on teachers, student teachers, and high school pupils had shown that most of the individuals possess average or low scientific attitudes.

It is interesting to see that the trend of scientific attitude in this sample of the study contradicts the above conclusion. This post adolescent student sample is better with regards to the possession of scientific attitude. Nearly 82% of the students sample possesses positive scientific attitude. From the pedagogic point of view it is to be considered as a good sign.

The socialization ability which is needed for proper functioning in the society, having its origins in the peer group, and class room also shows good signs. Thirty-nine per cent (39%) of the students show high socialization ability. This is also an indication that the process of schooling and education has contributed to the development of this ability. In this context it may not be out of place here to mention that the Indian student is in a social milieu where he is affected by conflicting variables. To quote a few of them are social structure, caste, religious, beliefs, etc.

In spite of the influence of the conflicting aspects the student population at this stage is found to be highly sociable.

But the variables chosen for this study and their influence

on the traits present an interesting picture.

The observation that the girls in the sample have better socialization ability needs to be discussed. Whether it is to be taken as a sign that the girl students are moving along with the changing society or this is an exclusive observation for this sample only deserves to be investigated further.

The variable co-educational condition in the class room producing higher socialization ability speak good of the educational institutions because most of them are co-educational.

The current fancy in the educational system in Andhra Pradesh at junior college level is admitting the students in residential junior colleges. The students is exposed to a strict discipline to which he is not accustomed to and he is put into a strict academic routine, well maintained study hours, eating hours, and recreational hours. But the present study points out that students in non-residential educational system show better socialization ability. The investigator humbly suggests that educationists should debate this point. This conclusion is not meant to speak against the residential system at junior college level. The Government of Andhra Pradesh is now encouraging and running residential junior colleges and most of the student population is getting attracted to the residential system at this stage. The parents also spend heavy amounts to provide residential education to their children. In this state the residential system of education has come to stay. It is going to be a salient feature of education at the junior college level.

When most of the student population is going to study in residential system it is necessary that this important aspect, namely, developing socialization ability should also be taken care of by the system. It is suggested that a more detailed study of the socialization practices, socialization activities, student grouping are studied with reference to the residential system.

The fact that all the five variables chosen for this study, namely, discipline, medium of learning, sex, class room conditions, and type of institution are not influencing the scientific attitude in this sample of student population. It is also encouraging to know that arts and science students show same level of scientific attitude and there are no differences in scientific attitude between boys and girls.

Regarding attitude towards science it is but natural that

science students hold more favourable attitude. But the observation that students learning in non-co-educational institutions hold more favourable attitude towards science needs further investigation. But, on the whole this sample of student population holds favourable attitude towards science speaks good of school and home as agencies for developing this attitude.

The fact that a high percentage of this sample is identified as possessing positive scientific attitude gives scope for discussion about science education received by them. As a matter of fact in this sample of junior college students six per cent (6%) is possessing high positive scientific attitude and seventy-six (76%) per cent is possessing positive scientific attitude. On the whole 82% of the sample is identified as possessing positive scientific attitude. This by itself is significant.

But on the basis of this figure the investigator is not taking the liberty of commenting on the science education received by them in lower classes, because of the criticism levelled against the science curriculum and science teachers in Indian Schools.

Science is made a compulsory subject up to class ten level due to its multifarious advantages. To teach such a useful subject lively, and meaningfully, we need efficient and effective science teachers. The quality of science teaching mainly depends on the quality of its teacher, but neither on the facilities available nor on the richness of the content. Unfortunately many of our schools are equipped with the science teachers who lack in—

- necessary teaching and manipulative skills
- scientific attitude, creativity, and originality
- interest either in teaching or in the future of children and the state
- adequate knowledge in subject and the latest happenings around the world
- appropriate pre-service or in-service training
- the idea of allowing children to grow in physical and mental capacities spontaneously.

We do not, of course, blame the teachers alone. Our school children too will also not cooperate in effective teaching-learning process. In this regard too, the teacher have a role to play in moulding their clientele according to their requirements.

The investigator is not concluding, that in spite of the science curriculum, science teacher, and the science teaching conditions in the schools, the students have developed scientific attitude.

It is possible that there are some schools with good facilities for science teaching, there are some good science teachers who provide good learning experiences in sciences for their pupils. But some of the studies on Scientific attitude have shown that experienced science teachers are low in scientific attitude, most of the schools are poorly equipped for science teaching.

In this context, the scope for developing scientific attitudes in pupils in the schools, is a distant possibility. So when school is not a possible agency for developing scientific attitude, then what are the real agencies that have developed scientific attitudes in this sample of junior college students? Probably, it is the home, the environment, the mass media, and the peer group that have contributed to this. It was already pointed out that the development of attitudes through these agencies is not done in a planned manner. The outcomes are due to daily interaction.

It is to be assumed that the Indian home, social environment, peer group, and mass media are reflecting the impacts of technological progress and resulting in a logical thought process which is being called scientific attitude.

This once again leads to the basic argument that through science teaching conscious attempts for developing scientific attitude are to be made. Science teaching with emphasis on product and process approaches, can help the individual acquire the functional science concepts needed in the modern society, help in understanding the processes of science leading to the development of scientific attitude and simultaneously result in the development of a positive attitude towards science.

Incidentally, another interesting aspect of this study is that only 54% of this sample of junior college students displayed favourable attitude towards science. To interpret it in the context of the scientific attitude of this sample, is difficult because all those holding positive scientific attitude can be expected to hold favourable attitude to science. Probably, this is a display of the conservative streak of Indian society which is still in the midst of modernization.

But the sample through its scientific attitude, has shown that they are objective, rational, curious, open minded, free from superstitions, and are able to suspend their judgement. To conclude the investigator proposes the concept of indirect trait relationship between socialization abi'' y, scientific attitude, and attitude towards science among post adolescent college students. This relationship is evident in post adolescent college students. There are also reasons to believe that common agencies are helping in the development of these traits, the chief among them appears to be the peer group, the home, and mass media.

The role of a school as an agency in developing scientific attitude and attitude towards science needs to be thoroughly investigated. The above proposed explanation can be investigated with reference to different populations like pre adolescent students, university students, and students in professional courses like engineering, medicine, and law, etc.

SUGGESTIONS FOR FURTHER RESEARCH

The present study which was conducted with hypothesis of a triangular relationship between the traits (1) socialization ability (2) scientific attitude, and (3) attitude towards science, with the assumption of common origins for their growth and development makes the investigator give the following suggestions for further studies in this area:

1. Since value system is also an outcome of school, home, society and peer group, a study of socialization ability and its relation to value system and value preferences of post adolescent students will be useful.
2. A study of the socialization practices in residential and non residential junior colleges can be taken up.
3. A study of socialization ability and scientific attitude of pre-adolescents, i.e., end of schooling will yield useful data.
4. A study of socialization ability, value system, and scientific attitude of teachers, can be taken up.
5. Identification of traits and the agencies influencing them especially with reference to values, scientific attitude, and democratic attitude towards environment can be taken up.

6. Development in the verification of socialization strategies for classroom implementation is needed.
7. The investigator is of the opinion that a more detailed study of the association between the traits socializatior ability and scientific attitude is needed.
8. Studies on the correlation between these two traits using factorial techniques may give an in-depth view of trait relationships.
9. A study of the components of scientific attitude and its association with socialization ability is needed because scientific attitude consists of different components like rationality, curiosity, aversion to superstitions, objectivity of intellectual beliefs and suspended judgement.

6

Executive Summary

THE PROBLEM AND ITS SIGNIFICANCE

Education is a process through which the inborn qualities or latent powers of the child are improved and unfurled, so that his personality is developed.

It is important that education has to take into account the social aim also. The social values, mores and milieus make the individual socialized.

Socialization can be defined in terms of the learning process associated with interaction between persons. It is also defined as an interacting process between the individual and his environment, through which, the individual becomes a person.

As such, socialization is a process which is of value both to the individual who gets socialized, and the group which socializes him. Further, socialization is a continuous process. It begins from the moment the child becomes responsive to his environment and goes on till the end of his life. It is pronounced in completely new social situations and groups.

The process of socialization takes place in two ways :

(a) deliberate and

Development of social conformity, social adjustment, social intelligence, and positive moral character are the important factors involved in socialization.

Social conformity takes two forms—acquiescence and conventionality. Conformity becomes stronger in adolescence. At that time, the opinions of others especially of one's own age group, are of immense importance.

Social adjustment among adolescents and youths is measured by degree of popularity in the peer group. It means achieving satisfactory status with his peers. The school as a socializing agency, helps the children in achieving the social adjustment.

Taking the role of another person or putting one self into the other, is sometimes referred to as "social intelligence".

Social competency or social intelligence plays an important role in the kind of social adjustment the adolescent makes. It gives the adolescent poise and self confidence, traits that are of great value in any social situation.

Ultimately, much of child's social behaviour (and an adult's to) is determined by ethical ideas about what is right and what is wring.

These needs, aspirations and goals of life of a society are realized through a number of organizations like the home, the religious institution, the school, the youth clubs, the mass media, etc., called as agencies of education. These are organisations of a society, which preserve and perpetuate social customs traditions, beliefs, values, etc., while satisfying the primary needs of an individual.

There are two types of agencies, namely, formal and informal. There are innumerable agencies of socialization either spontaneously formed or set up deliberately in the society. School is an important agency of socialization to serve certain individual and societal needs which are originally designed and established by the society.

The most important developmental task of adolescence according to Erikson, is the search for and the achievement of sense of identity. Becoming independent of parents and gaining acceptance of peers are important steps in achieving a sense of personal identity.

Late adolescence occurs between fifteen to eighteen years. The young adolescent has three 'social worlds' which are of equal importance to him. The first consists of his family. Many of the social contacts for work and play are with his parents, brothers and sisters, and other relatives. The school provides the second social world for the young adolescent, while the third consists of a small closed world of intimate friendship with one or two individuals of his sex, whom he regards as his 'best friends' and with whom he associates in many of his activities and with whom he shares his thoughts, hopes and worries.

Socialization inculcates basic disciplines ranging from toilet habits to the methods of science. Socialization disciplines impulsive behaviour through social approvals and disapprovals. Socialization instils aspirations.

It is through socialization that the individual becomes aware of and learns the roles he has to play in the society. Socialization teaches the basic skills of social life. Socialization creates a 'self-image'. Socialization develops a 'we-feeling', a sense of belongingness to a group. Socialization is one of the important functions at all levels.

Education has to be the chief instrument of society in cleaning the social life of undesirable norms. The combined influences of school-cultural demands, the home situation, the social class status, and other forces in the adolescent environment operate to produce a well adjusted or poorly adjusted personality.

By studying friendships in adolescence we can better understand the various aspects that contribute to their complex social maturation. The adolescent period is every critical in terms of social adjustments and maturation. The adolescent's physical and psychological development, attitudinal developments, his ambitions, development of value system may in turn be affected by the socialization process he has undergone. The peer group and school may have greater influence on him than home.

Selecting or choosing good friends and proper social interaction with them develops socialization ability in adolescent, which can show an automatic solution for all the adolescent problems. The persons who have proper social intelligence develop social skills necessary to overcome this identity crisis.

Failure in socialization can lead to different forms of delinquency.

An attitude denotes an adjustment of the individual towards some selected person, group or institution. An attitude results in a state of preparation or a state of readiness to respond in a particular manner under particular circumstances. Attitudes may be formed towards persons or group of persons; towards the products of human interaction. Since the attitude of members of the social group toward a person moulds his self-attitudes, the person who experiences favourable social attitudes, can be expected to be self-acceptant.

Attitudes may be referred to as sociogenic motives. Attitudes arise out of the socialization of an individual in a group. During the period from 12 to 30, most of the person's attitudes take final form and thereafter change little. This has been called the critical period, the period during which attitudes crystallize. During this period three main factors are at work: peer influences, information from mass media and other sources, and education.

Of all the adolescent's attitude developments, attitude towards science and scientific attitudes are important and useful. The scientific attitude represents the motivation which converts the knowledge of facts and skills in the use of scientific method into action and refers to the 'willingness' to use scientific procedures and methods. It may best be described as "an attitude to ideas and information to particular ways of evaluating them" a formulation which distinguishes it from 'an attitude to science or scientists' on one hand and from 'an ability to carry out scientific procedures' on the other.

The scientific attitude is applicable to nearly every situation an individual may encounter in the process of acquiring knowledge in life situations. It is closely allied to critical thinking, and it is developed through the study of science as well as other subject matter areas.

The scientific attitude as it appears in the literature of science education embodies the adoption of a particular approach for solving problems, for assessing ideas and information or for making decisions. Using this approach evidence is collected and evaluated objectively, so that the idiosyncratic prejudices of the one making the judgement do not intrude. All available evidence is carefully weighed before the decision is made. If the evidence is considered to be insufficient, then judgement is suspended, until there is enough information to enable a decision to be made. A person to follow this procedure is said to be motivated by the scientific attitude and is generally conceived by science educator as some one who makes decisions solely on the basis of the weight of empirical evidence.

The proper development of scientific attitude is possible mainly through conscious attempts during science teaching. By adopting scientific attitudes and, transferring these to situation in every day life, students can be expected to be more tolerant of other's point of view and to be more successful in living and working along side with other people. The study of science also gives opportunity for the development of favourable traits of human character.

The architect of the modern world is science. The most important of all the reasons for learning science is that it has a value in character training. Every literate person needs to develop and possess a positive attitude to science.

Once the child is being socialized in a proper manner, he knows how to live in this world. In addition to socialization, advancement of knowledge is another important aim of education. Only when the person is having a proper attitude towards science, he can aspire to be a knowledgeable person. He also realises and appreciates the fundamental principles of science which are essential to effective living in today's world. Hence, to have a proper attitude towards science is very important and this may also be required for socializing the individual.

Every individual needs socialization ability, positive attitude towards science and a better level of scientific attitude. They are useful for effective functioning in the society. Scientific attitude is an outcome of science education. Science, when it is taught in a democratic and social atmosphere is known to help in the development of scientific attitude. Positive attitude to science is developed through education, media, and technological social environment.

The importance of the three traits, common social components, common origins necessitates a combined study of these three traits in post adolescent students. With the assumption of association of these three traits, studies on student population are necessary.

An individual with high scientific attitude is likely to possess positive attitude towards science and vice versa. A individual with high scientific attitude is likely to possess high socialization ability and vice versa. An individual with high socialization ability is likely to possess positive attitude towards science and vice versa.

These traits are always being affected by many factors in different stages. For example, personality traits, attitude towards science, scientific attitude, socialization holding on to a value system are some of the traits which influence the growth and development of adolescents.

In spite of the known natural fact that most of the traits tend to develop normally, it is also seen that when a trait is influenced by certain factors, or a trait is being consciously developed through the process of education in an individual then there is every probability that trait distribution will not be normal in that population. If the traits have grown in the same arena or of same origin then they may be developed in a planned manner.

A knowledge of relationship between the traits will be educationally useful because it may result in developing classroom strategies, help in planning proper co-curricular activities. It can also help in developing guidance principles for adolescents.

As attitudes are always functional and also emotionally satisfying, similarity of attitude may be one of the important determinant of socialization. It will be very useful to know whether there is any relationship between socialization ability and attitude.

If socialization ability has a direct relationship to scientific attitude, then there is every possibility to improve the socialization ability of the child through scientific attitude. One can find out the common measures to be followed to improve both. Hence there is a need for the study of this area.

With the knowledge of social structure of the class and group, it will be possible for a teacher to plan to change the student's attitude.

It is of utmost importance to know this association in an adolescent. The structure of adolescent group is likely to be much more complex than that of groups of younger children. Different degrees of social acceptance may have different effects on adolescent attitudes.

In this period positive moral characterization also takes place. For this, an adolescent should have proper attitudes, and knowledge skills also, apart from other skills. By knowing the association between socialization ability, the attitude especially scientific attitude and attitude towards science; it may be possible for the teacher to improve the socialization ability, develop scientific attitude and attitude towards science in more planned manner.

The junior college students are in the stage of late adolescence. They are in the age group of seventeen plus. These adolescent college students are at a crucial stage in their life. They possess all the characteristics of adolescents and are passing through the adolescent crisis.

They are in a process of developing moral character, developing different tastes and interests. They have aspiration and attitudes.

These students have completed five years of primary schooling and five years of high school education. They received science education during all these ten years, both in primary and high school levels.

The students may also develop some general characteristics during this educational stage.

The nature of science education and way it is imbibed by the individual, can be influencing his attitude towards science and scientific attitude. The study proposes to focus its attention on knowing the nature of and relationship between socialization ability, scientific attitude and a attitude towards science.

Further, the focus is on identifying the influence of the following variables; sex, type of institution, medium of learning, class environment and discipline on the three dependent variables of the study.

For the purpose of this the investigator decides to make a study of socialization ability, scientific attitude and attitude towards science among junior college students who are in late adolescence.

In order to make an investigation of the three traits, among college students and their nature of association the following research questions were framed.

1. *How are the traits socialization ability, scientific attitude and attitude towards science distributed in junior college students?*
2. *In the chosen population, is there any association between these traits?*

The following are the objectives framed.

1. *To identify the trend of distribution of the socialization ability in junior college students.*
2. *To find out the attitude the students have towards science.*
3. *To find the scientific attitude of junior college students.*
4. *To study the association among the three traits, namely:*
   a. *Socialization ability*
   b. *Scientific attitude*
   c. *Attitude towards science*
5. *To study the variable wise association among the three traits, namely:*
   a. *Socialization ability*
   b. *Scientific attitude*
   c. *Attitude towards science*
6. *To identify the influence of the following variables on socialization ability, scientific attitude, and attitude towards science in junior college students.*
   a. *Sex*

b. *Type of Institution*
c. *Medium of Learning*
d. *Class Environment*
e. *Discipline*

METHOD OF INVESTIGATION

A review of related studies and literature enabled the investigator to choose the method for conducting this study. Since this investigation comes under descriptive category of study, it was felt that 'Survey method' will help in gathering the data needed to answer the research questions.

Tools

As already pointed out the traits to be measured from the sample are socialization ability, scientific attitude, and attitude towards science. While the latter two can be measured by using paper and pencil tools i.e. attitude scales. The measurement of socialization ability has to be undertaken by using 'sociometric technique'. The tools selected for the study are described below.

Sociometric questionnaire to find out the socialization ability of the student was used. The researcher devised the sociometric questionnaire on the basis of the guidelines and the sample items given by J.L. Moreno (1939). It consists of four questions having three choices for each question. The questions were based on the two aspects. The group of pupils who like one another. The group of pupils who reject one another. Sociomatrices are drawn for each section separately. From the sociomatrices, pupil's sociometric scores were noted. According to the pupil's sociometric scores (total number of choices), pupils were classified into six categories. They were popular, above average, average, below average, neglectees, isolates and rejectees.

The researchers selected scientific attitude scale constructed and standardised by J.K. Sood and R.J. Sanadhya. The scale contained thirty-six statements, of which eighteen are of positive polarity and eighteen are of negative polarity.

To measure attitude towards science the investigator has used the Science Attitude Scale by Avinash Grewal (1977) there are twenty statements in this scale.

The three questionnaires, namely, Sociometric Questionnaires,

Science Attitude Scale, and Scientific Attitude Scale, were administered to 15 groups comprising of 446 pupils.

Sample

Socialization ability can be measured in the context of a group only, the investigator had to resort to the technique of random selection of 15 groups of 8 junior college students.

The area which is chosen for this investigation for sociometric analysis, is an urban area. Education wise, there are a number of junior colleges offering education at this level, in both residential and non residential systems. They provide instruction in Mother tongue and English also. The student population is mostly non-local with students coming to study the Intermediate course from various towns and villages. In all, the city has twenty-nine junior college; Fifteen groups of Intermediate students were randomly selected from the above twenty-nine junior colleges. The groups were of varied sizes depending on the number of students in that class.

To enable the investigator to answer the research questions regarding the distribution of the three traits in the sample and to find whether there is association between the traits, the following declarative hypotheses were chosen.

Hypotheses

- *I.* *The traits socialization ability, scientific attitude, and attitude towards science will be distributed normally in this sample of junior college students.*
- *II.* *The traits socialization ability, scientific attitude and attitude towards science will be associated with each other in this sample.*
- *III.* *In all the sub-samples of junior college students there will be association between the three traits socialization ability, scientific attitude, and attitude towards science.*
- *IV.* *The variable selected for the study, namely, Sex, Class Environment, Medium of Learning, Type of Institution, and Discipline will be the influencing variables of the three traits--socialization ability, scientific attitude, and attitude towards science.*

Statistical Procedure

1. *The level of significance chosen for interpreting the values is 0.01 level.*
2. *Score distributions are classified into categories. For attitude, classification like highly negative, negative, neutral, positive, and highly positive were used for socialization ability, categories like popular, isolates, etc., were used.*
3. *Chi-square test of significance is used to verify normality of distribution and Test of Independence of traits.*
4. *For identifying the influencing variables, t-test was applied for comparing the mean differences in the sub-sample.*

CONCLUSIONS

The main assumption of this study was that, in this sample of post adolescent junior college students, all the three traits will be associated with each other.

The analysis of data led the investigator to draw the following conclusions.

1. All the Three Traits are not Distributed Normally

a. The Traits Socialization Ability is not Distributed Normally

The socialization ability scores, which are expected to be distributed normally along the scale 'Isolate' to 'Populars', are differing significantly from the expected situation. The trend of socialization ability scores is skewed towards the 'Above Average to Popular' categories. This suggests, this sample of junior college students acknowledge the importance of the process of socialization by identifying certain fellow students as being above average or popular.

This trend is probably because the junior college students do not like to work in isolation, rather they work in groups, move in groups, sit together and even dine together.

This sample of junior college students have their preferences to most of their classmates, as their seating, working, and eating companions, resulting in more of above average and populars in this sample. Hence, a significant percentage of the sample shows high socialization ability.

b. The Trait of Occurrence of Scientific Attitude is not Distributed Normally

The trend of occurrence of scientific attitude scores is towards positive scientific attitude, than normally expected. This suggests, this sample of Junior college students have acquired better scientific attitude.

The scientific attitude is composed of rationality, curiosity, open mindedness, aversion to superstitions, objectivity of intellectual beliefs, and suspended judgement. Interestingly, these post adolescent students have very high level of curiosity.

Another significant characteristic of these students is their suspended judgement, which is one of the most important aspects of scientific attitude.

The sample of post adolescent students are more open minded and. are objective in their beliefs.

These students do seem to have objectivity of intellectual beliefs because, they know that evidence supporting a certain idea, should be provided, before the idea is accepted and that the scientists should draw inferences only on the basis of accurate observation.

The junior college students in post adolescent stage are rational, as they believe that an idea should not be accepted if it is proved to be poor and a conclusion based on insufficient evidence should neither be accepted nor be rejected.

Peculiarly, these students are not completely averse to superstitions. It is possible that over and above the effect of the peer group on the development of attitude towards science the deep rooted parental authority is contributing this to free themselves from superstitions.

The Indian home and the parents are well known for their deep rooted, inherent traditions which are full of superstitions carried from generation to generation and maintained within their community. But for this, the rest of the scientific attitude development in these post adolescent college students appears to be good.

c. Attitude Towards Science is not Distributed Normally

The trend of occurrence of attitude towards science score is towards moderate attitude than normally expected. This suggests that this sample of junior college students has moderate attitude towards science. When such large number of the junior college students show a positive level of scientific attitude, it is but natural to expect them to show a favourable attitude towards science. But only half of them admit that they hold favourable attitude to science. Peculiarly they did not have very strong attitude in this direction. They are aware that science sharpens ones reasoning power and logical thinking. It is noteworthy to observe that, for them, study of science subjects is not a dull affair and science provides more relationship than other subjects.

But, their other attitude responses towards science are more significant than the ones already pointed out. They think that science has made us to depend entirely on machines and admit that scientific knowledge alone cannot improve a man's life. They are afraid that science is bound to lead our society into godlessness. To them science subjects are very difficult to study. They think that science fails to solve all our problems. They believe that science alone is responsible for our progress. They are not sure whether scientific careers are more useful than other careers and almost admit that knowledge of science is not necessary for other subjects.

Another reason may be that the past academic environment, i.e., at primary and secondary levels is not helpful in developing a favourable attitude towards science. All the school subjects especially science and mathematics, contribute to the development of favourable attitude towards school subjects. Attitude towards science is an academic attitude. Similarly, all school subjects contribute to Scientific Attitude. Of course science and mathematics play a vital role, but language studies help in developing creativity, environment helps in widening the horizons of knowledge thus enabling the individual to be democratic, open minded, rational, secular, objective, accommodative, adjustable, and free from superstitions. While the school subjects seem to be developing these attitudes, which are a part and parcel of scientific attitude, it is surprising to note that the students are not favourably disposed to science subjects as a whole. Their feeling that science is difficult is a point worth analysing. It could be that the science class rooms are authoritarian. It could be that science teacher is not taking enough precaution to make the subject interesting or even developing a fear complex among the students by giving an impression that science is difficult.

It is suggested that a study of the Indian class rooms and teachers regarding the techniques and strategies they are using for developing favourable attitude towards various disciplines may throw some light.

II. In this sample, there is an association between the three traits, namely, socialization ability, scientific attitude and attitude towards science. But these are not directly associated with each other.

a. *As far as this sample of junior college students is concerned, there are evidences of association between socialization ability and scientific attitude.*
b. *There are no evidences of association between socialization ability and attitude towards science.*
c. *There are reasons to believe that, scientific attitude and attitude towards science are associated with each other in this sample.*

This raises the interesting question of why the students have positive scientific attitudes and do not have favourable attitude to science? There is no doubt that attitude towards science and scientific attitude are associated. The influence of science education, media, and teacher on the development of scientific attitude is well recognized. The students who are highly sociable are the products of primary and secondary education in our schools.

It is to be deemed that the present day school and society are successfully contributing to socialization and scientific attitude. For these students their peer groups are the nucleus of their society from which they relate themselves to the various societal aspects. Hence it is to be understood that these peer groups are functional, effective and contributory to the development of the students. The educational implications can be that the school, teachers and parents should know the dynamics of these peer groups. They should also be willing to identify the isolates and rejectees, find out the reasons and adopt remedial programmes.

Improvement in socialization ability may help the student to successively participate in the educational process for survival in the competitive world. The junior college student is in this stage of competition. He plans for future vocations. But again one has to come back to the question of why these students do not hold favourable attitude to science. Probably the traditional constraints in the society, social backwardness, religious influences on the individual or even the peer group influences may be the causes. Hence, this duality of attitudes regarding scientific attitude and attitude towards science.

Throughout the discussion it was evident that socialization ability, scientific attitude, and attitude towards science have common origins. All of them appear to be the outcomes of the process of social interaction which may be planned or unplanned. Peer group and socialization ability are interdependent scientific attitude is an outcome of social interaction in classrooms. Attitude towards science is an outcome of their exposure to science while acquiring socialization ability and scientific attitude. In spite of the discrepancy in attitude towards science and scientific attitude, all the three concepts of this study, seem to be socialogically interrelated. A more detailed investigation of sociological influences on these three aspects may throw more light on their origin and development.

Indian population has its leaning towards spiritualism and the present day Indian society is an amalgam of materialistic spiritualism and idealism. The population is still in the stage of developing and improving its attitude towards science. Hence the type and nature of attitude towards science held by Indian students cannot be similar to those held by their western counterparts. It has to be remembered that these students mostly belong to traditional backgrounds, and even if they are professing modernity, they lag behind in practising modernity. Modernization is known to influence the attitudes, and attitude towards science cannot be an exception to the influence of modernization process.

III. There are reasons to believe that the independent variables selected for the study are having influence on the distribution of the traits in sub samples.

a. *In all the sub samples of the variables the association of the traits socialization ability and altitude towards science is not evident.*

b. *Variation in the trait association in the sub-samples was found with reference to trait association between socialization ability and scientific attitude.*

The sub-samples in terms of medium of learning, sex, class environment and type of institutions indicate independent distribution of the traits socialization ability and scientific attitude. When the classification was in terms of discipline, trait association was found.

c. *Variation in trait association in the sub samples was found in trait association between scientific attitude and attitude towards science.*

The following sub samples showed association between scientific attitude and attitude towards science. They are: science students, students learning through Telugu medium, i.e., mother tongue, girls sample, boys sample, students in co-educational institutions, and sample of students from non-residential colleges.

Common variables were chosen for studying their influence on the traits.

a. *Of the five selected variables of the study, it is found that scientific attitude is not influenced by any one of them.*
b. *The variables, viz., discipline, sex, co-education, student's residential status were found to be influencing socialization.*

The findings are

i. Arts students show better socialization ability than science students.

Presumingly, the kind of education the person receives influences his socialization ability. Students who study arts subjects may be less rigid, less confirming and less authoritarian than those studying science subjects. As competition is more stiffer for science students than arts students it is obvious that they are more study oriented and career oriented. This may lead to the reduced social interaction, inter personal jealousies and probably there will not be close proximity among science students. These might have been the reasons for the better socialization ability of arts students than science students.

ii. Girls show better socialization ability than boys.

Girls tend to be voluble, share their secrets, generally converse in peer group and usually share their problems. Girls also have a tendency to confide in their friends whereas boys do not confide so easily. Even though boys mix in their peer group, they feel that they will be looked down if others come to know of their problems. So these boys try to avoid the group and become 'neglectees' or 'isolates' or even 'rejectees'. This may be the reason for the low socialization ability of boys than girls.

iii. Students of co-education institution show better socialization ability than students of uni-sex institutions.

In co-educational institutions boys and girls work together and this mixing of both the sexes makes them converse freely with each other. The atmosphere is free to do group work or for group interaction, whereas in unisex institutions, there may be less of interaction. Because of these reasons students of co-education institutions may be showing better socialization ability.

iv. Students of non residential institutions show better socialization ability than residential students.

Non-residential students or boarders spend their life together even after the college and they stay together during night time also. This close proximity may sometimes lead to rivalries. As this is the gang age, pupils band themselves together in groups and the prejudices and tensions involved may lead to group rivalries or clashes. Added to this there will be unhealthy competitions as they spend more time together. But day scholars have time to converse only during intervals and between the class hours, and time of interaction is less, and most probably there will be healthy conversation. This might have been the reason for better socialization ability of students of non residential colleges.

Students irrespective of their medium of learning generally converse in their mother tongue. Probably this might have been the reason for the above finding.

c. The trait attitude towards science is influenced by two variables, namely, discipline and class environment.

The findings are

i. Science students hold a more favourable attitude towards science than arts students.

The above finding is an obvious one.

ii. Students of unisex institutions are better than the students of co-

educational institutions as far as attitude towards science is concerned.

DISCUSSION

Post adolescent stage is a critical stage in the life of an individual. There, the 'individual is on the verge of the adulthood, ready to face the challenges of life, take up vocational responsibilities, and fulfill life aspirations. This stage is more stressful to the post-adolescent student who is on the verge of planning for vocational education. For Indian students this stage in their educational career occupies highest significance. Along with his ambitions he has to fulfil the parental ambitions, compete with the general student population, compete within the peer group, and come out successfully in life.

Psychologically speaking, the socialization ability of an individual and qualities like applying scientific method, to personal and day to day problems can be helpful to the individual in successfully passing through this phase.

Educationists are of the opinion that socialization ability and the scientific attitudes are useful assets to an individual. Parallely the favourable attitude towards technological changes which are the outcomes of science—otherwise called as favourable attitude towards science can also be an asset to the individual.

There is no doubt that the socialization ability of an individual mainly develops in the school and peer group. The scientific attitude is developed both in the school and the home. The attitude towards science is developed as an outcome of liking towards science subject, vocational ambitions in the field of science, and maybe to a certain extent peer group influence. Thus the development of scientific attitude as contributed by the school is mainly through learning of science and home influence where convention and traditions are followed and religious beliefs are learnt and practiced.

In the Indian context there is always a clash between science and religion. The population is generally believed to have low scientific attitudes. It is not out of the way to point out that the scientific attitude studies on teachers, student teachers and high school pupils had shown that most of the individuals possess average or low scientific attitudes.

It is interesting to see that the trend of scientific attitude in this sample of the study contradicts the above conclusion. This post adolescent student sample is better with regards to the possession of scientific attitude. Nearly 82% of the students sample possesses positive scientific attitude. From the pedagogic point of view it is to be considered as a good sign.

The socialization ability which is needed for proper functioning in the society, having its origins in the peer group, and class room, also shows good signs. Thirty-nine (39%) of the students show high socialization ability. This is also an indication that the process of schooling and education has contributed to the development of this ability. In this context it may not be out of place here to mention that the Indian student is in a social milieu where he is affected by conflicting variables. To quote a few of them are social structure, caste, religious, beliefs, etc.

In spite of the influence of the conflicting aspects the student population at this stage is found to be highly sociable.

But the variables chosen for this study and their influence on the traits present an interesting picture.

The observation that the girls in the sample have better socialization ability needs to be discussed. Whether it is to be taken as a sign that the girl students are moving along with the changing society or this is an exclusive observation for this sample only deserves to be investigated further.

The variable co-educational condition in the class room producing higher socialization ability speak good of the educational institutions because most of them are co-educational.

The current fancy in the educational system in Andhra Pradesh at junior college level is, sending the students to residential colleges. The student is exposed to a strict discipline to which he is not accustomed to and he is put into a strict academic routine, well maintained study hours, eating hours, and recreational hours. But the present study points out that students in non-residential educational system show better socialization ability. The investigator suggests that educationists should debate this point. This conclusion is not meant to speak against the residential system at junior college level. The Government of Andhra Pradesh is now encouraging and running residential junior colleges and most of the student population is getting attracted to the residential system at this stage. The parents also spend heavy amounts to provide residential education to their children. In this state the residential system of education has come to stay. It is going to be a salient feature of education at the junior college level.

When most of the student population is going to study in

residential system it is necessary that this important aspect, namely, developing socialization ability should also be taken care of by the system. It is suggested that a more detailed study of the socialization practices, socialization activities, student grouping are studied with reference to the residential system.

The fact that all the five variables chosen for this study, namely, discipline, medium of learning, sex, class room conditions, and type of institution are not influencing the scientific attitude in this sample of student population.

It is also encouraging to know that arts and science students show same level of scientific attitude and there are no differences in scientific attitude between boys and girls.

Regarding attitude towards science, it is but natural that science students hold more favourable attitude. But the observation that students learning in non co-educational institutions hold more favourable Attitude towards science needs further investigation. But on the whole this sample of student population holds favourable Attitude towards science speaks good of school, and home as agencies for developing this attitude.

The fact that a high percentage of this sample is identified as possessing positive scientific attitude gives scope for discussion about science education received by them. As a matter of fact in this sample of junior college students six per cent (6%) is possessing high positive scientific attitude and seventy-six (76%) per cent is possessing positive scientific attitude. On the whole 82% of the sample is identified as possessing positive scientific attitude. This by itself is significant.

But on the basis of this figure the investigator is not taking the liberty of commenting on the science education received by them in lower classes, because of the criticism levelled against the science curriculum and science teachers in Indian schools.

Science is made a compulsory subject up to class ten due to its multifarious advantages. To teach such a useful subject lively, and meaningfully, we need efficient and effective science teachers. The quality of science teaching mainly depends on the quality of its teacher, but neither are the facilities available nor on there is richness of the content. Unfortunately, many of our schools are equipped with the science teachers who lack in—

- *necessary teaching and manipulative skills*
- *scientific attitudes, creativity, and originality*

- *interest either in teaching or in the future of children and the state*
- *adequate knowledge in subject and the latest happenings around the world*
- *appropriate pre-service or in-service training*
- *the idea of allowing children to grow in physical and mental capacities spontaneously.*

We do not, of course, blame the teachers alone. Our school children too will also not cooperate in effective teaching-learning process. In this regard too, the teachers have a role to play in moulding their clientele according to their requirements.

The investigator is not concluding, that in spite of the science curriculum, science teacher, and the science teaching conditions in the schools, the students have developed scientific attitude. It is possible that there are some schools with good facilities for science teaching, there are some good science teachers who provide good learning experiences in sciences for their pupils. But some of the studies on scientific attitude have shown that experienced science teachers are low in scientific attitude, most of the schools are poorly equipped for science teaching.

In this context, the scope for developing scientific attitudes in pupils in the schools, is a distant possibility. So when school is not a possible agency for developing scientific attitude, then what are the real agencies that have developed scientific attitudes in this sample of junior college students ? Probably it is the home, the environment, the mass media, and the peer group that have contributed to this. It was already pointed out that the development of attitudes through these agencies is not done in a planned manner. The outcomes are due to daily interaction.

It is to be assumed that the Indian home, social environment, peer group, and mass media are reflecting the impacts of technological progress and resulting in a logical thought process, which is being called scientific attitude.

This one again leads to the basic argument that through science teaching conscious attempts for developing scientific attitude are to be made. Science teaching with emphasis on product and process approaches, can help the individual acquire the functional science concepts needed in the modern society, help in understanding the processes of science leading to the development of scientific attitude and simultaneously result in the development of a positive attitude towards science.

Incidentally another interesting aspect of this study is that only 54% of this sample of junior college students displayed favourable attitude towards science. To interpret it in the context of the scientific attitude of this sample, is difficult because all those holding positive scientific attitude can be expected to hold favourable attitude to science. Probably this is a display of the conservative streak of Indian society which is still in the midst of modernization.

But the sample through its scientific attitude, has shown that they are objective, rational, curious, open minded, free from superstitions and able to suspend their judgement. To conclude the investigator proposes the concept of indirect trait relationship between socialization ability, scientific attitude and attitude towards science among post adolescent college students. This relationship is evident in post adolescent college students. There are also reasons to believe that common agencies are helping in the development of these traits, the chief among them appear to be the peer group, the home, and mass media.

The role of a school as an agency in developing scientific attitude and attitude towards science needs to be thoroughly investigated. The above proposed explanation can be investigated with reference to different populations like pre-adolescent students, university students and students in professional courses like engineering, medicine, law, etc.

Bibliography

Alpern, Morris L. (1946), "The Ability to Test Hypothesis", *Science Education*, Vol. 30, Oct, pp. 220-29.

Atkinson, J. Myron and Burnold, Will R., *Encyclopaedia of Educational Research 4th Edition*, pp. 1192-205.

Atwater, Mary M. and Wiggins, John (1995), "A Study of Urban Middle School Students with High and Low Attitude Towards Science", *Science Education*, Vol. 79, pp. 1-6.

Austin, Mary C. and George, G. Thomson (1948), "Children Friendship—A study on the basis of which children select and reject their best friends", *Journal of Educational Psychology*, Vol. 39, pp. 101-16.

Bajpai, S.R. (1985), *Methods of Social Survey and Research* (12th Edition), Kitab Ghar, Kanpur, India.

Bajpeyi, S.K. (1971), *A Study of Sociometric Status of High School Students and Its Relation to Intelligence and Interest Patterns,* Third Survey of Research in Education, Edited by Buch, M.B., pp. 228-29.

Bandyopadhay, J. (1984), *Environmental Influence, Academic Achievement and Science Aptitude as Determinants of Adolescent Attitude Towards Science Stream,* Fourth Survey of Research in Education (1983-88), vol. I and II, NCERT, (1991).

Baron, D. (1951), "Personal—Social Characteristics and Classroom Social Status; A Sociometric Study of Fifth and Sixth Grade

Girls", *Sociometry*, Vol. 14, pp. 32-42.

Baumel, B. Howard and Berger, Joel J. (1965), "An attempt to Measure Scientific Attitudes", *Science Education*, Vol. 49, pp. 267-69.

Best, John. W. (1982), *Research in Education*, Prentice Hall of India Pvt. Ltd., New Delhi.

Bhalla, Shakuntala (1954), *Sociometry in a Classroom*, The Education Quarterly, Vol. 6, pp. 33-36.

Bhaskara Rao, D. (1982), *An Evaluative Study of the New Science Curriculum at Upper Primary Level in Andhra Pradesh*, Experiments in Education, Vol. X, pp. 147-49.

Bhaskara Rao, D., *et al*. (1986), *Scientific Attitudes of Experienced Science Teachers at Secondary School Level*, The Educational Review, Vol. XCII, pp. 60-65.

Bhaskara Rao, D. *et al*. (1989), *Scientific Attitudes and Personality traits of Prospective Science Teachers*, Progressive Educational Herald Vol. 3, pp. 66-66.

Bhaskara Rao, D. (1997), *Scientific Attitude*, Discovery Publishing House, New Delhi.

Bhaskara Rao, D. (1997), *Reflections on Scientific Attitude*, Discovery Publishing House, New Delhi.

Bhaskara Rao, D. (1998), *Adolescence Education*. Discovery Publishing House, New Delhi.

Bonney, E. Merl (1942), *A Study of Social Status on the Second Grade Level*, Journal of Genetic Psychology, Vol. 60, pp. 271-305.

Bonney, E. Merl (1948), *A Study of Friendship Choice in College in Relation to Church Affiliation In-Church Preferences, Family size and length of Enrolment in College*, Journal of Social Psychology, Vol. 29, pp. 153-66.

Brubacher, John. S. (1969), *Modern Philosophies of Education*, Fourth Edition, Tata, McGraw Hill Publishing Co. Pvt. Ltd., New Delhi.

Buch, M.B. (Ed) (1979), *A Survey of Research in Education*, Society, M.S. University, Baroda.

Buch, M.B. (Ed) (1979), *Second Survey of Research in Education*, Society for Educational Research and Development, Baroda.

Buch, M.B. (Ed) (1987), *Third Survey of Research in Education*, NCERT, New Delhi.

Buch, M.B. (Ed) (1993), *Fourth Survey of Research in Education,* NCERT, New Delhi.

Byson, L. Barrington and Byson, Handricks (1989), "Attitude towards Science and Science Knowledge of Intellectually Gifted and Average Students in Third, Seventh and Eleventh Grades", *Journal of Research in Science Teaching,* Vol. 25 (8), pp. 679-87.

Caldwell, O.W. and Gerhard E. Lundun. (1931), "Students Attitudes Regarding Unfounded Beliefs", *Science Education,* Vol. 15, pp. 246-66.

Cattell, B. Raymond (1934), "A Psychological Study of Character and Temperament", *Character and Personality,* Vol. 3, pp. 53-54.

Chandratre, R. (1982), *A Study of the Self Image of Adolescents in Relation to their Sociometric and Socio-Economic Status,* as cited in 3rd Survey of Research in Education, M.B. Buch (Ed) (1987), pp. 338-39.

Chaube, S.P. (1983), *Adolescent Psychology,* Vikas Publishing House Pvt Ltd., New Delhi.

Chauhan, S.L. (1982), *Sociometric Correlates of Self Concept* as cited in 3rd Survey of Research in Education, M.B. Buch (Ed.) (1987).

Cherylmason and Jane, Butler Kahle (1988), "Student Attitudes towards Science and Science Related Carriers : A Program Designed to Promote a Stimulating Gender Free Learning Environment", *Journal of Research in Science Teaching,* Vol. 26 (1), pp. 25-39.

Chowdary, Aparajitha, *et. al.* (1997), *Sociometric Status and Development of Self Concept in Elementary School Children,* Experiments in Education, Vol. XXV (1)

Clifford T. Morgan (1978), *A Brief Introduction to Psychology* (2nd Edition) Tata McGraw Hill Company Ltd., New Delhi.

Cox, F.N. (1953), *Sociometric Status and Individual Adjustment before and after Play Therapy,* Journal of Abnormal Social Psychology, Vol. 48, pp. 354-56.

Croft, I.J. and Grygier, T.J. (1956), *Social Relationships of Truants and Juvenile Delinquents,* Human Relations, Vol. 9, pp. 439-66.

Crow, Lester D. and Crow, Alice (1956), *Human Development and Learning,* Eurasia Publishing House (Pvt.) Ltd., Ram Nagar, Delhi.

Cot Grove, Stephen (1975), *the Science of Society,* George Allen & Unwin Ltd., London.

Darely, John. G., *et. al.* (1951), "Studies of Group Behaviour, Stability, Change and Inter Relations of Psychometric and Sociometric Variables", *Journal of Abnormal and Social Psychology,* Vol. 46, pp. 565-76.

Davids, A. and Parneti, A. Anita (1958), "Time Orientation and Interpersonal Relations of Emotionally Disturbed and Normal Children", *Journal of Abnormal and Social Psychology,* Vol. 57, pp. 299-305.

Davis, C. Ira (1935), *The Measurement of Scientific Attitudes,* Science Education, Vol. 19, pp. 117-22.

Dewey, John, (1963), *Democracy and Education, Macmillan,* New York.

Dhundiyal, N.C. (1984), *A Study of the Effects of Teacher Expectations of the Sociometric Status of Primary Grade Pupils,* 4th Survey of Research in Education, M.B. Buch Ed. (1993), pp. 1268.

Dorothy, L. Gabel, Peter, A. Rubba and Franz, R. Judy (1977), *The Effect of Early Teaching and Training Experience on Physics Achievement, Attitude towards science and Science Teaching and Process Skill Proficiency,* Vol. 61, pp. 503-11.

Dunnigton, Margaret J. (1957), *Investigation of Areas of Disagreement in Sociometric Measurement of Pre-School Children,* Child Development, Vol. 28, pp. 93-102.

Ediger, Marlow and D. Bhaskara Rao (1996), *Science Curriculum,* Discovery Publishing House, New Delhi.

Education Policies Commission (1966), *Education Spirit of Science,* Washington, D.C. National Education Association.

Evans, K.M. (1961), *Sociometry and Education,* Routledge and Kegan Paul, London.

French, R.L. and Mensh, I.N. (1948), *Some relationships between interpersonal judgement and sociometric status in a college group,* Sociometry, Vol. 11, pp. 335-45.

French, R.L. (1951), *Sociometric Status and Individual Adjustment Among Naval Recruits,* Journal of Abnormal Social Psychology, Vol. 46, pp. 64-72.

Fuller, Elizabeth M. and Helen, B. Baune (1951), *Inquiry Proneness and Adjustment in a Secondary Grade : A Sociometric Study,* Sociometry,

Vol. 14, pp. 210-25.

Garden, Lindzey and Ellcot, Armson (1975), *The Hand Book of Social Psychology, (*2nd Edition), Amerind Publishing Company Pvt. Ltd., Delhi.

Garret, H.E. (1985), *Statistics in Pshchology and Education,* Eleventh Indian Reprint, Vakils, Feffer and Simons Ltd., Bombay, India.

Garrington, Karl C. (1956), *Psychology of Adolescence,* Fifth Edition, Prentice Hall Inc., Englewood Cliffs, N.J., U.S.A.

Gauld, Colin F. and Hawkins, A.D. (1980), *the Scientific Attitude: A Review,* Studies in Science Education, Vol. 66, pp. 109-21.

German, Paul J. (1988), *Development of the Attitude towards Science in School Assessment and its use to Investigate the Relationship between Science Achievement and Attitude towards Science in Schools,* Journal of Research in Science Teaching, Vol. 25(8), pp. 689-703.

German, Paul J. (1995), *Testing a Model of Science Process Skill Acquisition, An Interaction with Parents Education, Preferred Language, Gender, Science Attitude, Cognitive Development, Academic Ability and Biology Knowledge,* Science Education, Vol. 79. pp. 1-6.

Ghosh, B.N. (1984), Scientific Methods and Social Research, Sterling Publishers (Pvt.) Ltd., New Delhi.

Green, T.L. (1954), Studies of Inter-Group Relations in Ceylon, Education and Psychology, pp. 27-35.

Grewal, Avinash (1977), Manual for Science Attitude Scale, National Psychology Corporation, Raja Mandi, Agra.

Gronlund, N.E. (1955), *The Relative Stability of Clussroom Social Status with unweighted and weighted Sociometric Choice*, Journal of Educational Psychology, Vol. 46, p. 345-54.

Grossman, Beverly and Wrighter, Joy (1948), *The relationship between selection-rejection and intelligence, social status and personality among sixth-grade children*, Sociometry, Vol. 11, p. 346-55.

Guilford, J.P. and Fruchter (1978), *Fundamental Statistics in Psychology and Education*, Tata McGraw Hill Company, Pvt. Ltd., Delhi.

Haladyna, Tom, *et. al.* (1982), *Relations of Student, Teacher and Learning Environment Variables to Attitudes towards Science*, Science Education Vol. 66, pp. 673.

Haney, E. Richard (1984), *The Development of Scientific attitudes*, The Science Teacher vol. 32, p. 33-35.

Harty, Samuel, Beall (1988), *Relationship among the Constructs of Attitude towards Science, Interest in Science, Curiosity and self concept of Science Ability,* Science Education, Vol. 72, pp. 308.

Heiss, Eldwood D., Ellsworth S. Obourn and Charles W. Hoffman (1950), *Modern Science Teaching,* New York, The Macmillan Co., Delhi.

Henry, N.B. (Ed.) (1960), The fifty-ninth year book of the National Society for the study of Education, part I; Chicago.

Hollander, E. P. (1964), *Leaders, Groups and Influence,* Oxford University Press.

Hopkins, K.D. and Stanley, J.C. (1928), *Educational and Psychological Measurement and Evaluation,* Prentice Hall of India Pvt. Ltd., Delhi.

Hurlock, B. Elizabeth (1973), *Adolescent Development,* McGraw Hill Kogakuska Ltd., Tokyo.

Hurlock, B. Elizebeth (1986), *Personality Development,* Tata McGraw Hill Publishing Company Ltd., New Delhi.

Jamod, S.K. (1982), *Social Relations of the Boys Studying in Primary Schools of Bavnagar,* Fourth Survey of Research in Education, M.B. Buch (Ed.) (19893) pp. 153.

Jaya Kumari, S. (1991), "Social Rejection Scale Preparation", *Indian Journal of Applied Psychology,* Vol. 28(1), the Madras Psychological Society.

Jaya Prasad Rao (1976), *The Instrument of Social Change,* Education India, Vol. XVII, No. 7, January.

Joshi, H.O. (1980), *Sociometric Study of the Star and Isolate Girls,* III Survey of Research in Education, M.B. Buch (Ed.), (1987), pp. 142-43.

Kanga, D.D. (1949), *Where Theosophy and Science Meet: A Stimulus to Modern Thought,* Vol. I. (Second Edition), The Adyar Library Association, Madras.

Kaur, D. (1985), *An Investigation into the sociometric structure of secondary school teachers as studied with their students liking for them and analysed with some psychometric variable,* Fourth Survey of Research in Education, M.B. Buch (Ed.), (1993), pp. 951.

Kelly (1988), "A Longitudinal Study of Students Attitude towards Science between ages 11 and 13 paying particular attention to variation by sex and social class", *Science Education*, Vol. 72, p. 137.

Kerkeurst, Arthur J. (1939), "The acceptance of superstitions beliefs among secondary school pupils", *Journal of Education Research*, Vol. 32, pp. 673-85.

Korde, Ashok and Sawant, Ankush (1980), *Science and Scientific Method*, (Science, Technology and Development), (Fourth Edition), Himalaya Publishing Company, Bombay.

Krishna, D.G. (1975), "A Study of Scientific Attitude and Its Relations to Intelligence of Graduate Students", Unpublished Master of Education Dissertation, Andhra University, Visakhapatnam, A.P., India.

Kuhlen, R.G. and Bretsch, H.S. (1947), "Sociometric Status and Personal Problems of Adolescents", *Sociometry*, Vol. 10, pp. 122-32.

Kulkarni, B.G. (1975), *An Investigation into Attitude of Pupils, Parents and Teachers towards Work Experience*, Third Survey of Research in Education, M.B. Buch (Ed.), (1987)., p. 543.

Kuppuswami, B. (1977), *An Introduction to Social Psychology*, Asia Publishing House, Pvt. Ltd.

Kuppuswami, B. (1980), *A text took of Child Behaviour and Development*, (2nd Revision Edition) Vikas Publishing House pvt. Ltd., Delhi.

Laudis, H. Paul, *Adolescence and Youth*, pp. 373-85.

Laybourn and Bailey (1971), *Teaching Science to the Ordinary Pupil*, (Second Edition), the English Language Book Society and University of London Press Ltd., London.

Lemann, T.B. and Solomon, R.H. (1952), *Group Characteristics as Revealed in Sociometric Pattern and Personality Ratings*, Sociometry, vol. 15, pp. 7-90.

Lindzey, G. and Goldwyn, R. (1954), *Validity of the Rosenweig Picture—Frustration Study,* Journal of Personality, Vol 22, pp. 519-47.

Lindzey, G., and Urdan, J.A. (1954), *Personality and Social Choice,* Sociometry, Vol. 17, pp. 47-63.

Madhosh, A.G.W. (1982) *Personality Correlates of Sociometric Status in Different Inter Personal Situation,* third Survey of Research in Education, M.B. Buch (Ed.). (1987) pp. 373.

Malhotra, Sudha (1969), *Interpersonal Relationship: Psychological, Socio-*

logical and Educational Study, United Publishers, Allahabad, India.

Marja, Talvi and D. Bhaskara Rao (1996), *Educational Leadership and Social Change*, Discovery Publishing House, New Delhi.

Marks, J.B. (1954), *Interest, Leadership and Sociometric Status Among Adolescents*, Sociometry, Vol. 17, pp. 340-49.

Mead, G.H. (1934), *Mind, Self and Society* as cited in "Introduction to Social Psychology by B. Kuppuswami, pp. 347.

Mills, C.R. (1953), *Personality Patterns of Sociometrically Selected and Sociometrically Rejected Male College Students*, Sociometry, Vol. 16, pp. 151-67.

Mishra, B.N. (1981), *The Relationship between personality traits and sociometric choices in Classroom*, Third Survey of Research in Education, M.B. Buch (Ed.), pp. 377-78.

Misti, Frank, L. Jr., *et al.*, (1991), *Science Attitude Scale for Middle School Students*, Science Education, Vol. 75, pp. 525-40.

Mohanthy, J. (1986), *Indian Education in the Emerging Society*, 3rd Edition, Sterling Publishers Private Ltd. New Delhi.

Mollie, S. Smart, *et al.*, (1967), *Children Development and Relationships*. The Macmillan Company, London.

Moshin. S.M. (1984), *Research Methods in Behavioural Sciences*, Orient Longman Ltd., Delhi.

Murthy, S.K. (1982), *Teacher and Education in Indian Society*, A treatise on Philosophical and Sociological Foundations of Education, Prakash Brothers 4th ed, Ludhiana.

Musgrave, P.W. (1979), *The Sociology of Education*, Third Edition, Metheun and Company, London & New York.

Nagar, S. (1973), *A Comparative Study of the Personality characteristics of socially accepted and rejected girls of higher secondary schools of Agra City*, II survey of Research in Education, M.B. Buch (Ed.) (1979), p. 188.

Nalini Rao (1975), *School as a precussor of child's social milieu*, Educational India, Vol. XVI, No. 7, January.

National Policy of Education—1986 (With Modifications undertaken in 1992) Ministry of Human Resource Development, Department of Education, Publication, No. 1723, New Delhi.

National Science Teacher's Association (1971), *School Science Education for the 70's*, The Science Teacher, 38(8), pp. 46-51.

Noll, Victor, H. (1935), *Measuring the Scientific Attitude*, Journal of Abnormal and Social Psychology, Vol. 30, pp. 145-64.

Northway, Marg, L. (1940), *A Method for depicting social relations obtained by sociometric testing*, Sociometry, Vol. 7, pp. 10-25.

Northway, Mary, L. and Blossom, T. Widger (1947), *Rorschach Patterns related to the sociometric status of social Children*, Sociometry, Vol. 10, pp. 186-99.

Owen, C.B. (1964), *Method for Science Masters*, The English Language Book Society and Macmillan and Co. Ltd., London.

Patel, K. (1975), *An Investigation of Sociometric Variables and their Correlates in Multi Lingual Nursery Children Attending Anglo-Indian Schools*, II Survey of Research in Education, M.B. Buch (Ed.) (1979), pp. 225-26.

Pathak, R.D., *Sociometric Status and Adjustment Level in School Children*, III Survey of Research in Education, M.B. Buch (Ed.) (1987), p. 393.

Paulline V. Young, Calvin F. Schmid and Panly, N.R. (1968), *Scientific Social Surveys and Research*, Prentice Hall of India Pvt. Ltd., (4th Edition), New Delhi.

Pearson, Karl (1900), *Grammar of Science as cited in Science and Religion* by Swami Ranganathanada, Mayawati, p. 6.

Pillai, Kamala S. (1987), *Interactive Effect of Science Aptitude and Attitude towards Science of Biology Achievement*, Journal of Educational Research, Vol. II(2).

Pruthi, S. and Nabi, S.A. (1991), *Scientific Literacy and Democracy A Case Study of the Attentive Public*, Journal of Scientific and Industrial Research, Vol. 50, pp. 589-95.

Rathaiah, L., D. Bhaskara Rao and Paturi Koteswara Rao (1997), *Achievement Correlates*, Discovery Publishing House, New Delhi.

Rathaiah, L. and Digumarti Bhaskara Rao (1996), *International Innovations in Education*, Discovery Publishing House, New Delhi.

Ravindranath, M.J. (1983), *Development of Scientific Attitude: An Experimental Study*, Journal of Indian Education, pp. 28-32.

Rebecca, V.P. (1976), *A Study of Ethnic group influences on socialisation of Primary School Children in age group 8-12 yrs in the city of Mysore*, II Survey of Research in Education, M.B. Buch (Ed.), (1979), pp. 121-22.

Reilly, Mary St. Anne, *et al.* (1960), *The Complimentary of Personality needs in friendship choice*, Journal of Abnormal and Social Psychology Vol. 61, pp. 290-94.

Richardson, J.E. and Forestor, J.F. (1951), *Studies in the Social Psychology of Adolescent*, Routledge & Kegan Paul Ltd., London.

Ross, James S. (1962), *Group work of Education Theory*, George Harrap & Sons, London.

Salodkar, M.P. (1987), *A comparative sociometric study of leadership choice tendencies of certain social organisation as related to education*, Fourth Survey of Research in Education, M.B. Buch (Ed.) (1993), p. 191.

Sandrette, Onas C. (1958), *Social Distance and Degree of Acquaintance*, Journal of Education Research, Vol. 51, p. 367.

Say, A. (1986), *Process of Socialization and its impact on personality formation in a Tribal Village of Chotanagpur*, Fourth Survey of Research in Education, M.B. Buch (Ed.), (1993), pp. 195.

Schibeci, R.A. and Riley, J.P. (1986), *Influence of students background and perceptions on science attitudes and achievement*, Journal of Research in Science Teaching, Vol. 23(3), pp. 177-87.

Secord, Paul P. (1978), *An Introduction to Social Psychology*, Tata McGraw Hill Publishing Co. Ltd., New Delhi.

Sharma, A. (1970), *Handbook on Sociometry: For teachers and Counsellors*, NCERT, New Delhi.

Sharma, J.N. (1978), *Manual for Sociometry*, Agra Psychological Research Cell, Agra, India.

Sharma, M. (1974), *A Study of Correlates of Sociometric Status in High School Classes*, IInd Survey of Research in Education, M.B. Buch (Ed.) (1979), p. 128.

Sharma, R.A. (1992), *Fundamentals of Education Research*, (3rd Ed.), Loyal Book Depot, Meerut, India.

Sharma, R.C. (1981), *Modern Science Teaching*, Dhanpat Rai & Sons, Delhi.

Shrivastava, N.N. (1983), *A Study of the Scientific attitude and its measurement*, Indian Educational Review, Jan, pp. 95-97.

Simpson, D. Ronald and Steve J. Oliver (1990), *A Summary of Major Influences on Attitude towards and Achievement in Science among adolescent students*, Science Education, Vol. 74(1), pp. 1-18.

Singh, Daljit Inder (1980), *A Sociometric study of Self esteem among High School Children.*

Smelser, N. (1952), *Sociometric structure and its correlates: Social class background and courtship—marriage attitudes*, Unpublished honours thesis, Harvard University, Lindsey.

Sorenson, Herbert, *Psychology in Education*, (1st Edition), McGraw Hill Book Company, New Delhi.

Steve, Oliver J. (1988), *Influences of Attitude towards science, Achievement motivation and science self concept on achievement in science, A longitudinal study*, Science Education, Vol. (72).

Subrahmanyam, C. (1976), *Science and Spiritual Values*, Educational India, Vol. XLIV, No. 5, November, Editor: M. Venkatarangaiya.

Sudha, Kumari (1982), *A Study of Intelligence, Achievement, Adjustment and Socio Economic Pattern of Different Sociometris Groups of Adolescents*, 4th Survey of Research in Education, M.B. Buch (Ed.), (1993), p. 391.

Sudhir, M.A. and Darchhingper, N. (1987), *Science Achievement and Science Attitude Among College Students*, Journal of Institute of Education Research, Vol. II(3).

Swami Budhananda (1992), *Can one be Scientific and Yet be Spiritual*, Advaita Ashram, Calcutta.

Swami Pavitrananda (1989), *Modern Man in Search of Religion* (Seventh Ed.), Advaita Ashram, Calcutta.

Swami Ranganathanand (1982), *Science and Religion*, Advaita Ashram, Calcutta.

Swarnamma, G. (1978), *An Inquiry into the Teaching of Biology in the Upper Primary Schools of Kerala*, III Survey of Research in Education, M.B. Buch (Ed.) (1987), pp. 568-69.

Tagiuri, R. (1952), *Relational Analysis: An Extension of Sociometric Method with Emphasis upon Social Perception*, Soociometry, Vol. 15, pp. 91-104.

Taton, Simpson (1988), *Relationship of Self, Home and Classroom Environment with Attitudes towards Science*, Science Education, Vol. 72, p. 308.

Taneja, V.R. (1987), *Socio-Philosophical approach to Education*, Atlantic Publishers & Distributors.

Tamar Levin, Naama Sabar and Ziporalibman (1991), *Achievement and*

Attitudinal Patterns of Boys and Girls in Science, Journal of Research in Science Teaching, Vol. 28(4), pp. 315-28.

Tunkikorn, T. (1988), *Attitudes towards Science and Achievement in VII, VIII, IX grades in Science Classes in Thailand*, Science Education, Vol. 72, p. 307.

Upamanyu, V.V. (1974), *An Investigation into the Relationship Between the Socio-Metric Status and Different Components of Anxiety*, III Survey of Research in Education, M.B. Buch (Ed.) (1987), p. 133.

Vaidya, Narendra (1976), *The Impact of Science Teaching*, Oxford & IBH Publishing Co., Delhi.

Vessel (1965), *The Library of Education: Elementary School Science Teaching*, Prentice Hall of India (Pvt) Ltd, Delhi.

Vreeland, M. Francis and Stephen, M. Corey (1936), *A Study of College Friendship*, Journal of Abnormal and Social Psychology, Vol. 30, pp. 229-36.

Wareeng, Carol (1991), *A Survey of Antecedents of Attitudes towards Science*, Journal of Research in Science Teaching, Vol. 27(4), pp. 371-88.

Watson, Goodwin (1966), *Social Psychology and Issues*, J.B. Lippincott Company, Philadelphia.

Young, Pauline V. and Schmid, Calvin. F. (1968), *Scientific Social Surveys and Research*, (Fourth Ed.), Prentice Hall of India Pvt. Ltd., New Delhi.

APPENDIX—A

Scientific Attitude Scale

Instructions

The following statements are concerned with Scientific attitude. Read each statement carefully and then mark your answer on the sheet. Work rapidly. Record your first impression, the feeling that comes to your mind, as you read the item.

Draw a circle around SA if you strongly or fully agree with an item. Draw a circle around A if you are in partial agreement with the item. Draw a circle around N if you are neutral, Draw a circle around D if you partially disagree. Draw a circle around SD if you strongly or totally disagree. Answer all statements.

1. Now it is not possible to develop more sensitive x-ray machine. SA A N D SD

2. To challenge the Bible that the sun revolves round the earth was not the right step of Copernicus. SA A N D SD

3. A conclusion based on insufficient evidences should neither be accepted nor be rejected. SA A N D SD

4.	An idea should not be accepted if it is proved to be poor.	SA	A	N	D	SD
5.	The Scientists should have to find out the occurrences of the undesired events in nature.	SA	A	N	D	SD
6.	The ideas are true if few facts support them.	SA	A	N	D	SD
7.	Scientists should be curious to find out the occurrences of the undesired events in nature.	SA	A	N	D	SD
8.	Every novel situation should not be viewed in an interrogate war.	SA	A	N	D	SD
9.	After observing the astonishing situations like magic, a person should not strive to know the secret of it.	SA	A	N	D	SD
10.	Until they achieve success, the scientists should continue their efforts in collecting complete information about the Mars.	SA	A	N	D	SD
11.	Scientists shall be able to forecast the sex of a foetus in future.	SA	A	N	D	SD
12.	Science students should be eager to conduct new experiment.	SA	A	N	D	SD
13.	A senior scientist should not accept the new technique suggested by another.	SA	A	N	D	SD
14.	One scientist should not give the right to another scientist to defy his established law.	SA	A	N	D	SD
15.	Positive criticism benefits the advancement of knowledge.	SA	A	N	D	SD
16.	The scientist B should modify his erroneous concepts if scientist A presents	SA	A	N	D	SD

the correct and fully tested facts before him.

17.	In perspective of new discoveries and inventions, a scientist should be ready to change his prevalent conceptions.	SA	A	N	D	SD
18.	People should be willing to change the ideas if sufficient evidences about the hollowness of their ideas are available.	SA	A	N	D	SD
19.	It is impossible to defy widely held assumption in society since very long time.	SA	A	N	D	SD
20.	We should not believe that small pox, cholera and other diseases are the products of (divine) anger.	SA	A	N	D	SD
21.	If one sneezes at the time of commencing a new task, one should start it later.	SA	A	N	D	SD
22.	Cooked stories by astrologers and magicians should not be preferred to scientifically based explanations.	SA	A	N	D	SD
23.	For weather predictions, magicians and astrologers should not be consulted.	SA	A	N	D	SD
24.	A scientist should not start his work when the way is crossed by a cat.	SA	A	N	D	SD
25.	At the time of drawing inferences the scientist should draw only those conclusions which concide with the present political ideologies.	SA	A	N	D	SD
26.	Unacceptable new idea by all people should not be given due consideration.	SA	A	N	D	SD
27.	Enough evidence supporting a certain idea should be provided before that idea is accepted.	SA	A	N	D	SD

28.	People should read only those news papers which are in consonance with their political ideologies.	SA	A	N	D	SD
29.	The scientist should draw inferences on the basis of accurate observation.	SA	A	N	D	SD
30.	If a tea company offers a bribe to any scientist, then he should not disclose the research finding about the adverse effects of tea.	SA	A	N	D	SD
31.	Knowledge once accepted should not be put to test.	SA	A	N	D	SD
32.	When traditional beliefs are in conflict with scientific discoveries, it is better to accept the traditional beliefs.	SA	A	N	D	SD
33.	Due to fast explosion of knowledge, facts and theories which stand true to-day may be disproved tomorrow.	SA	A	N	D	SD
34.	Although a new theory propounded by a senior and experienced "Scientist A" raised some doubts in the minds of a junior and young "Scientist B". Then "Scientist B" should accept "Scientist A" theory.	SA	A	N	D	SD
35.	More importance should be given to the traditional beliefs than the new dis-coveries of science.	SA	A	N	D	SD
36.	If a science teacher fails to arrive at the expected results during demonstration, he should try to discuss the possible cause of his failure.	SA	A	N	D	SD

APPENDEX—B

Science Attitude Scale

Directions

Given below are some statements about science. Some of these statements describe how you might feel about science. We are interested in knowing your valuable opinion about science as a subject of study. You may agree with some of these statements and you may disagree with others. After you have read a statement carefully, decide whether or not you agree with it.

If you agree strongly with statement put a circle around the category SA (Strongly Agree) if you agree put a circle around A (Agree), if you are undecided put a circle around U (Undecided), if you disagree put a circle around D (Disagree), and if you strongly disagree put a circle around SD (Strongly Disagree).

You are requested to give your free and frank opinion.

1. Scientists are persons without human considerations. SA A U D SD
2. Scientific careers are more useful to the society than other careers. SA A U D SD
3. Study of science subjects is rather a dull affair. SA A U D SD

4.	Other subjects cannot be properly understood without the knowledge of science.	SA	A	U	D	SD
5.	Science subjects are very difficult to study.	SA	A	U	D	SD
6.	Science subjects are more exact than others.	SA	A	U	D	SD
7.	Science bound to lead our society into godlessness.	SA	A	U	D	SD
8.	Science subjects provide more relation than other subjects.	SA	A	U	D	SD
9.	Scientific knowledge alone cannot improve a man's life.	SA	A	U	D	SD
10.	Science sharpens our reasoning power and logical thinking.	SA	A	U	D	SD
11.	Science fails to solve all of our problems.	SA	A	U	D	SD
12.	Science subjects are useful for getting a success in the competitive examination.	SA	A	U	D	SD
13.	Too much emphasis on science would bring down our moral standards.	SA	A	U	D	SD
14.	Science alone is responsible for our technical and industrial progress.	SA	A	U	D	SD
15.	Study of science makes one realise the danger in misuse of scientific knowledge.	SA	A	U	D	SD
16.	Working in a scientific field bring more fame.	SA	A	U	D	SD
17.	Science can be studied by males only.	SA	A	U	D	SD
18.	Science subject open up many avenues of employment.	SA	A	U	D	SD

19.	Science has made us to depend entirely on machines.	SA	A	U	D	SD
20.	Science has turned the impossibilities into possibilities.	SA	A	U	D	SD